— FUN WITH —
CHINESE CHARACTERS
The Straits Times Collection ①

Cartoonist: Tan Huay Peng

FEDERAL PUBLICATIONS

An imprint of Times Media

Published for The StraitsTimes
by Times Media Private Limited

© 1980 Federal Publications (S) Pte Ltd
© 2000 Times Media Private Limited
A member of the Times Publishing Group
Times Centre
1 New Industrial Road
Singapore 536196
E-mail: fps@corp.tpl.com.sg
Online Book Store: http://www.timesone.com.sg/te

First published   1980
Reprinted   1982 (twice), 1983 (twice),
                   1985 (twice), 1986, 1987 (three times),
                   1988 (three times), 1989, 1990, 1991 (four times),
                   1992 (three times), 1993, 1994 (four times)
                   1995 (three times), 1996, 1997 (three times),
                   1999, 2000 (twice)

ISBN 981 01 3004 X

Printed by Press Ace Pte Ltd

INTRODUCTION

The genesis of the Chinese script is lengthy and remote. Very little of its history and origin is known to us as there is a lack of documentary evidence. Of the various legends concerning the creation of the Chinese script, the comparatively acceptable legend says that it was Cāng Jí 倉頡, a minister of the Emperor Huáng Dì 黄帝 , who first invented the script. It was the outcome of an extraordinary occasion on which Cāng Jí observed the footprints of birds and beasts whose lines and shapes were distinct and discernible. Deeply inspired by the sight of this, he then drew the pictures of the objects in accordance with their shapes and forms. These pictures of the primitive age were further reduced to the essentials, conventionalized and in time highly stylized. In other words, they were reduced for the sake of simplicity to a few lines. These picture characters were often, especially in their archaic forms, very expressive and were called **xiàng xíng** 象形 , literally "image shapes" by the Han lexicographer Xǔ Shèn 許慎 (30A.D.–124A.D.); or "pictography" by many a contemporary paleographer. In some cases, however, the so called "picture characters" were distorted beyond recognition. It is understandable that concrete objects such as phenomena of nature, man and his attributes, animals and plants, tools and implements and so forth are easily drawn and admirably adapted to represent language. Here are some examples:

For representation of phenomena of nature, there were such pictographs as rì "sun" ☉ 日 日 , yùe "moon" ☽ ☽ 月 , the older the forms of the characters, the closer the resemblance between the characters and the objects. The characters shuǐ "water" 水 水 (also abbreviated as three drops of water 氵 when it functions as a determinative) and chuān "stream, river" 巛 川 were drawn as flowing water in a stream or river. The character shān "mountain" ⛰ ⛰ 山 is a clear, faithful picture of a string of hills, and the same may be said of the character yǔ "rain" 雨 雨 雨 which is expressed by drops of water falling from heaven.

A great number of pictographs relate to man and his attributes. The character rén "man" 人 人 人 人 人 was represented by a simple linear picture depicting a variety of manners in which a man might appear. For nǚ "woman" 女 女 and mǔ "mother" 母 母 , there were picture characters depicting the humble, kneeling and gentle manners of the fair sex. The two dots on the body of the latter symbolized the breasts of a mother. There were picture characters which symbolized the eye "mù" 目 目 目 , ear (ér) 耳 耳 , hand (shoǔ) 手 手 手 (also abbreviated as 扌 when functioning as a determinative) and mouth (koǔ) 口 口 etc.

The world of animals was also widely represented. We have such quadrupeds as hǔ "tiger" 虎, yáng "sheep" 羊, xiàng "elephant" 象, mǎ "horse" 馬 and quǎn "dog" 犬 (also abbreviated as 犭 when functioning as a determinative). As for birds, the script distinguishes between niǎo (ordinary bird) 鳥 and zhuī (short-tailed bird) 隹. In addition, there was yet another picture, wū "crow" 烏, with the omission of a dot from the head of an ordinary bird.

There were pictographs that denote plants and fruits. For instance, mù (tree) 木 highlighted the branches and roots of a tree; caǒ (grass) 艸 depicted the upward shooting of buds, while zhú (bamboo) 竹 described the dangling leaves of a bamboo tree; guǒ (fruit) 果 was a picture of the tree that bore fruit. So was the picture character mǐ (rice) 米 depicting grains of rice on top of a plant.

There were numerous pictures which bore witness to the growth of civilization in ancient China. Take a look at the characters for tools and implements; for instance, dāo (knife) 刀, chē (cart, chariot) 車, zhoǔ (broom) 帚, mǐng (bowl) 皿, hú (wine vessel) 壺, yú (spirit vessel) 酉, cè (document, book) 冊, yù (brush) 聿 and wǎng (net) 网 (abbreviated as 罒) and so on.

The pictographs, which were to a certain extent comparable with the hieroglyphic characters, later evolved into the kind of characters which Xǔ Shèn called "zhǐ shì" 指事, literally "pointing to matters". In the West it was variously called "indirect symbols" or "indicative symbols". Whatever term philologists might call them, these characters were ingeniously adapted by early inventors to render abstract ideas. As a result, the scope of Chinese script was further widened.

The methods of creating such ideographs were many: the drawing of a meaningful symbol, the addition of a sign to a pictograph, making parts stand for wholes, attributes for things, effects for causes, instruments for activities, gestures for actions, to mention just a few. In a nutshell, the abstract ideas were rendered in a metaphorical or symbolic way. For example, by drawing one line: 一, two lines: 二, three lines: 三 or four lines: 亖 (this ideograph is no longer in use now) the early inventors meant yī (one), èr (two), sān (three) or sì (four) respectively. By adding a dot or a line onto the horizontal line: 上 (now 上) or below it: 下 (now 下), he meant shàng (up, above) or xià (down, below) respectively. Similarly, by adding a stroke to the top of the pictograph "木" tree (一 十 木 = 末), or to the lower part of it (一 十 木 = 本), he meant mò (top branches, end of a branch) or běn (root, trunk) respectively.

While a horizontal stroke stood for yī (one), a vertical stroke 丨 was then taken to mean shí (ten). It was later corrupted into 十. A vertical line down the centre of a circle signified zhōng (centre, the middle) φ 中 . A hand drawing a bow and arrow, needless to illuminate, meant shè (to shoot with a bow) 𝆏 𝆏 射. Similarly, to thrust at a person with a spear could but mean fá (to attack) 𝆏 𝆏 伐 . A man with crossed legs symbolized the notion of jiāo (to cross, connection) 𝆏 交 ; so did the picture of a standing man unmistakably represent the idea of lì (to stand) 𝆏 𝆏 立 .

As civilization advanced, rapid social changes took place. Things became so complicated that the hieroglyphic characters or the ideographs could no longer suffice for the expression of massive abstract notions. Just as the proverb said, "Necessity is the mother of invention", a kind of phonetic script, called **"xíng shēng"** 形 声 by Xǔ Shèn, or better known as "determinative-phonetic characters", was invented. The method of inventing determinative-phonetic characters was quite simple and yet most ingenious that the Chinese scribes could and still can invent new characters in unlimited numbers. Because of this, the growth of Chinese script had never been so rapid and before long the determinative-phonetic characters excelled the pictographs and the ideographs in rendering the language and thereafter they became the dominant class of characters in the Chinese script. The evolution of the Chinese script to this stage could be regarded as complete, and almost all the existing Chinese characters, except for five per cent or so, are of this sort.

This new method of creation might be viewed as a kind of phonetic writing which must, however, not be taken for an alphabetic script. It was simply the combination of a determinative indicating or suggesting the sense of the word and a phonetic indicating or suggesting the pronunciation of the word. The following examples will serve to explain how this simple, convenient and progressive method works:

Determinative	Phonetic	Compound
水 shuǐ (water; abbrev. 氵)	+ 其 qí (his, her, its, this, that; originally winnowing basket, now 箕) .	= 淇 qí (the River Qí)
玉 yù (jade; abbrev. 𤣩)	+ 其 qí	= 琪 qí (a valuable white stone or gem)
木 mù (tree; wood)	+ 其 qí	= 棋 棊 qí (Chinese chess)

石 shí (stone) ... + 其 qí = 碁 qí (another variant of 棋 which was made of stone)

馬 mǎ (horse) ... + 其 qí = 騏 qí (a piebald horse)

鹿 lù (deer) ... + 其 qí = 麒 qí (a fabulous, auspicious animal)

鳥 niǎo (bird) ... + 其 qí = 鵸 qí (a kind of wild goose)

月 yuè (moon; time)
{ + 其 qí = 期 qí (a period of time; a fixed date; expect to)
+ 其 jī = 期朞 jī (a full year; anniversary)

欠 qiàn (owe; deficient) ... + 其 qí = 欺 qī (to cheat; to oppress)

心 xīn (heart) ... + 其 jì = 惎 jì (to poison; to hate)

土 tǔ (earth; land; ground) ... + 其 jī = 基 jī (foundation; base)

竹 zhú (bamboo; abbrev. ⺮) ... + 其 jī = 箕 jī (a winnowing basket)

屮 cǎo (grass; abbrev. ⺿ now 草)
{ + 其 jī = 萁 jī (a kind of grass)
+ 其 qí = 萁 qí (the stem of bean)

示 shì (an omen; to manifest; abbrev. 礻) ... + 其 qí = 祺 qí (fortunate; lucky)

糸 mì (the archaic form of 絲 silk) ... + 其 qí = 綦 qí (dark grey; superlative)

蟲 chóng (worm; abbrev. 虫) ... + 其 qí = 蜞 qí (part of the word 蟛蜞 which is a kind of crab)

+ 其 qí, jī or jì = ...

The examples cited above were a series of words with the same (or approximately the same) pronunciation that could be written down with no possibility of confusion or misunderstanding at all. Thus 其 qí or jī or jì is always a phonetic, never a determinative in a compound word, though it is also the character representing such words as his, her, its, their, this, that, etc., in its own right. We may cite another series of examples in which the character 木 mù (wood) is nearly always a determinative of a compound word showing that almost all the words, which amount to 1,585 included in the largest Chinese dictionary, have something to do with wood:

Determinative		Phonetic		Compound	
木 mù (wood)	+ 卜	·bo (final particle)	= 朴	pò (a kind of oak: Quercus dentata; also the simplified form of 樸)
	+ 卜	·bo (final particle)	= 朴	pō (an old knife-shaped weapon)
	+ 卜	bǔ (to divine; to foretell)	= 朴(樸)	pú (simple and plain)
木 mù (wood)	+ 土	tǔ (earth; land; ground)	= 杜	dù (the russet pear; to shut out; to stop; to prevent)
木 mù (wood)	+ 反	fǎn (to turn over; to rebel; to turn back)	= 板	bǎn (board; blocks for printing)
木 mù (wood)	+ 木	mù (wood)	= 林	lín (forest; grove; copse)
木 mù (wood)	+ 公	gōng (public; open to all)	= 松	sōng (the pine tree; loose)
木 mù (wood)	+ 同	tóng (together; same; alike; and; with)	= 桐	tóng (a name applied to various trees e.g. sterculia platanifolia)
木 mù (wood)	+ 每	měi (each; every)	= 梅	méi (plums; prunes)
木 mù (wood)	+ 票	piāo (warrant; bill; ticket)	= 標	biāo (mark; beacon; signal; flag; notice)
木 mù (wood)	+ 黃	huáng (yellow)	= 橫	héng (crosswise; horizontal; side way)
木 mù (wood)	+ 匱	guì (cupboard; wardrobe)	= 櫃	guì (cupboard; wardrobe; shop-counter)
木 mù (wood)	+ 闌	lán (door-screen)	= 欄	lán (railing; animals' pen)
木 mù (wood)	+ 雚	guàn (heron; small cup)	= 權	quán (weight; power; authority)
木 mù (wood)	+ 覽	lǎn (look; inspect)	= 欖	lǎn (the Chinese olive)
木 mù (wood)	+ 登	dēng (to rise; to mount)	= 橙	chéng (orange)

A further 1,550 such examples may be added to the list, if we wish, of which the character 木 mù is always a determinative though it is the pictograph for wood itself. Furthermore, 木 mù can also function as a phonetic in the compound 沐 mù (to wash; to bathe; to cleanse; to enrich by kindness; to receive favours; etc.). Hence, apart from the fact that every pictograph and ideograph can be used as a phonetic, certain such pictures and symbols can be determinative as well. Since the number of determinatives was comparatively small, a radical system was devised to use the determinatives as a convenient means of classifying the characters in dictionaries. The first great dictionary *Shuō Wén Jiě Zì* 说文解字 of Xǔ Shèn, which was completed in 121 A.D., recognized 540 radicals, or bù shǒu 部首, in all. This number remained unchanged until the imperial dictionary *Kāng Xī Zì Diǎn* 康熙字典 of the Ching Dynasty (1644 A.D.–1911 A.D.) reduced it to 214, at which they still remain today.

As time went on, the Chinese language, as with all other languages, underwent gradual changes. The phonetical change, in particular, of the language was so great that sound combinations which started almost identical and so could be fairly represented by the same phonetic became entirely unlike in the course of time. A typical example was the common phonetic 工 gōng (work; originally a picture of a carpenter's square) in the following determinative-phonetic characters: 功 gōng (merit; det. 力 lì "strength"), 訌 hòng (dispute; det. 言 yán "talk"), 红 hóng (red; det. 糸 mì "silk"), 扛 gāng (to carry; det. 手 shǒu "hand"), 杠 gāng (bench; det. 木 mù "wood"), 江 jiāng (river; det. 水 shuǐ "water") and 貢 gòng (tribute; det. 貝 bèi "shell, money") etc. They are hardly homophonous in modern Chinese even though they originally have one and the same sound. In particular, the cases of 扛 gāng, 杠 gāng, and 江 jiāng are even worse, for there is no similarity at all between the sound of the phonetic and that of the compound character.

Such are the primary structural methods of Chinese script which generally falls into three main categories in nature, namely pictographs, ideographs and determinative-phonetic characters described above. We may therefore call them sān-shū 三书 (three categories of script) instead of liú-shū 六书 (six categories of script) which were distinguished first by Liú Xīn 刘歆 and Xǔ Shèn in the latter Hàn Dynasty (25 A.D.–220 A.D.). As for the other three types of characters, namely huì yì 会意, literally "meeting of ideas" (**associative compounds or logical compounds**), zhuǎn zhù 转注, literally "transferable meaning" (**mutually interpretative symbols**) and jiǎ jiè 假借, literally "borrowing" (**phonetic loan characters**), they were classified neither in accordance with the structure nor with the nature, but with the usage of the characters.

Take the huì yì, associative compounds or logical compounds for instance, it is a sheer significant combination of two or more pictographs or ideographs so as to form a new character representing a new idea. Thus, 明 míng "bright" consists of the pictographs of 日 rì "sun" and 月 yuè "moon" (日 + 月 = 明); 鮮 xiān "fresh" consists of the pictographs of 魚 yú "fish" and 羊 yáng "sheep" (魚 + 羊 = 鮮); 好 hǎo "good; to love" consists of the signs for 女 nǚ "woman" and 子 zǐ "child" (女 + 子 = 好); 歪 wāi "awry; slanting" is a combination of the signs for 不 bù "not" and 正 zhèng "upright" (不 put on top of 正 = 歪); 尖 jiān "sharp point; tapering" is a combination of the signs for 小 xiǎo "small" and 大 dà "big" (小 put on top of 大 = 尖). Very interesting and expressive are such logical compound characters as 桑 sāng "mulberry tree" where many hands (叒) are picking leaves of a tree (木), and 男 nán "man" which shows someone employing his strength (力) in the fields (田) as opposed to 安 ān "peace; safety" which is the feeling of a woman (女) staying at home (宀). All these associative compounds differ from the determinative-phonetic characters in that the "resulting" sound of the compound has no relationship with the sound of any of the elements in the combination. The following set of equations may well serve to show the difference:

Huì Yì, Associative Compound

rì + yuè = míng

Xíng Shēng, Determinative-Phonetic Character

mù + qí = qí

A small category of Chinese characters whose significance has been very much debated is the so called zhuǎn zhù or mutually interpretative symbols. Apart from having the same determinative or bù shǒu 部 首 , these mutually interpretative symbols are synonymous in meaning and can be substituted for each other. This is a way of usage, not a method of structure, however. In reality, these characters consist of one indicator of sense i.e., the determinative and one indicator of sound i.e., the phonetic. Structurally, they belong to the determinative-phonetic characters.

The remaining category of Chinese characters, which is more or less a kind of phonetic characters, is known as jiǎ jiè or loan characters. As the term implies, this is not a structural classification either, but another way of linguistic usage. The method was as simple as to borrow the existing character of a homophonous word. For example, at the very inception of invention, there was no such character for the word laí "come", an idea difficult to depict. However, there had already been in existence a pictograph for a cereal plant 來 來 來 which homophonously sounded as laí. So the ancient scribes did a very easy and convenient task by borrowing the existent character 來 laí for the representation of the word laí "to come". Similarly, the pictograph 萬 wàn "scorpion" was borrowed to represent the word wàn "ten thousand". 其 qí "a winnowing basket" was borrowed to represent the word qí meaning "his", "her", "its", "their", "this" and "that". A very interesting example is the word xī "west", represented by this picture character 西 which originally meant that the bird was in the nest. Xǔ Shèn's reason for such a loan was that the bird rested in its nest at a time when the sun was setting in the west. It had therefore been borrowed to render the word xī "west". All these transferences occurred because they were homophones.

In short, the Chinese script can be structurally grouped into three categories, namely pictographs, ideographs and determinative-phonetic characters.

What we have just described above is about the structural evolution of the Chinese script. The course of such evolution is lengthy, yet it may be divided into the following four stages:

1.   **The Primitive Stage** (or **the Legendary Period**): this is the earliest stage of the Chinese script at which the pictographs originated from sheer pictures of objects. Although we have no direct archaeological evidence for this, Táng Lán 唐蘭 has nevertheless estimated that it must have been in existence for more than 10,000 years.

2.   **The Archaic Stage** (or **the Pre-Historic Period**): this is the stage of the ideographs which covers a period from the emergence to the completion of the indirect symbols. We have not only good reasons to believe, but also documentary evidence to prove that this happened about 5,000 – 6,000 years ago.

3.   **The Neo-Archaic Stage** (or **the Post-Historic Period**): this is the period of determinative-phonetic characters, which continued for a span of 1,600 years from the later Yīn Dynasty (1384 B.C. – 1112 B.C.) down to the Hàn Dynasty (206 B.C. – 220 A.D.). Almost all the materials of the ancient Chinese script that we now have belong to this long period. It was not only in this period that the Chinese script had completed its structural evolution, but towards the end of this stage, the Chinese script had gone through and finally completed its formal evolution as well.

4.   **The Contemporary Stage** (or **the Modern Period**):
As far as the development of the Chinese writing system is concerned, this is a stage of stability. Both the structural evolution and the formal changes could be said to have reached a state of perfection. Structurally, unlike the pictographs or the ideographs, the determinative-phonetic characters continued

to grow. Formally, however, after the appearance of the 楷書 kaǐ shū (standard script), which is still the normal script form and the basis of the printing form used today, some time in the period of Weì and Jìn Dynasties (221 A.D. – 580 A.D.), little formal changes had taken place ever since. It was not until the early 1950s that the Government of the People's Republic of China started to introduce a kind of simplified form for two thousand odd Chinese characters. This was done all for a very good cause of simplicity and convenience, but at a very handsome expense of damaging as well as distorting the beauty and logical structure of the Chinese script.

To sum up, the Chinese script had completed its structural evolution long before the beginning of the Western era. However, that does not mean that it ceased to grow thereafter. On the contrary, like the Chinese language it represents, it is a living as well as a metabolic system of writing, one of the most epoch-making inventions of mankind. Although many characters had become obsolete in the process of changes, new characters could be easily and simultaneously created for any newly arisen mass of events, things or notions because the Chinese had discovered a simple, convenient means of creating new characters.

Dr Ong Tee Wah
18 January 1980

(umbrella)

(duck)

(girl/woman)

(basket)

Peng

(person)

PREFACE

As a means of visual communication, Chinese written characters are fascinating in their ingenuity and originality. The earliest form of Chinese writing was **pictographic** – stylized pictures of objects. Graphic **symbols** supplemented pictographs to represent simple abstract thoughts. Later, for transmitting complex ideas, **ideographs** were created from already existing simple characters, conveying ideas by the juxtaposition of interchangeable elements.

To meet the demand for thousands of new characters, the Chinese resorted to **phonetic** or **harmonic** writing, relying on the radical for the sense and the phonetic for the sound.

Today, many complex characters have undergone **simplification** to facilitate writing by reducing the number of strokes.

Chinese characters are generally built up from 214 root characters or radical elements. These comprise the basic building blocks for innumerable compound characters. Some of these radicals or primitives are capable of standing independently as characters. Others function as components of compound characters. In combination, they assume variant or contracted forms. By understanding the basic meanings of the elements that form a character, it is possible to discern the significance of the whole character. Hence, the importance of studying the radicals.

This collection of cartoons introduces systematically the more commonly used radical elements and the compounds they build up, together with related or associated characters.

As a mnemonic aid, it analyses each character, tracing its evolutionary development from the original seal character to the regular and simplified forms.

Based on authoritative source materials, both Chinese and English, it draws inspiration from the lofty, yet down-to-earth, wit and wisdom of the Chinese mind. Above all, it takes an appreciative look at Chinese written characters through the imaginative and discerning eye of a cartoonist.

While every effort has been made to be as accurate as possible, strict precision of representation is by no means the overriding concern; for humour and delight has been given more than just an instrumental importance.

Originally published as a regular feature of The Straits Times Bilingual Page, it is now presented as a collection and an appetizer to introduce readers to the delightful and fascinating world of pictographs and ideographs.

Have fun, then, with Chinese characters!

CONTENTS 目录

105	岛	dǎo	123	谈	tán	141	禾	hé	159	胖	pàng
106	乌	wū	124	灰	huī	142	秋	qiū	160	有	yǒu
107	飞	fēi	125	灾	zāi	143	愁	chóu	161	来	lái
108	羽	yǔ	126	煽	shān	144	税	shuì	162	本	běn
109	习	xí	127	烧	shāo	145	秃	tū	163	体	tǐ
110	扇	shàn	128	黑	hēi	146	苏	sū	164	果	guǒ
111	鱼	yú	129	墨	mò	147	和	hé	165	课	kè
112	渔	yú	130	点	diǎn	148	年	nián	166	巢	cháo
113	鲁	lǔ	131	草	cǎo	149	甘	gān	167	末	mò
114	羊	yáng	132	苗	miáo	150	香	xiāng	168	未	wèi
115	鲜	xiān	133	叶	yè	151	牛	niú	169	妹	mèi
116	羔	gāo	134	花	huā	152	件	jiàn	170	姐	jiě
117	美	měi	135	茶	chá	153	牢	láo	171	爱	ài
118	义	yì	136	英	yīng	154	半	bàn	172	想	xiǎng
119	洋	yáng	137	竹	zhú	155	伴	bàn	173	忆	yì
120	羡	xiàn	138	笔	bǐ	156	告	gào	174	忘	wàng
121	火	huǒ	139	算	suàn	157	牧	mù	175	快	kuài
122	炎	yán	140	笑	xiào	158	肉	ròu	176	匆	cōng

女

nǚ
woman;
girl;
daughter

The original pictograph for woman depicted her in a bowing position ⏚ Apparently, for ease in writing, man reduced this to a humbler form — a woman kneeling down ⏚ — but not for long.
The modern version 女 graphically portrays the big stride woman has taken to keep up with man.

PENG

く　女　女

女儿	nǚ ér	daughter	
女工	nǚ gōng	woman worker	
女皇	nǚ huáng	empress	
女人	nǚ rén	woman	
女士	nǚ shì	lady	
女王	nǚ wáng	queen	
女性	nǚ xìng	the female	

女婿	nǚ xu	son-in-law
女子	nǚ zǐ	girl or woman
女朋友	nǚ péng yǒu	girl friend
女主角	nǚ zhǔ jué	female lead
女主人	nǚ zhǔ rén	hostess
妇女	fù nǚ	woman
子女	zǐ nǚ	children

Example:

我 们 的 工 厂 有 很 多 女 工 。
Wǒ mén de gōng chǎng yǒu hěn duō nǚ gōng.

It means, "Our factory has many woman workers."

1

子 **zǐ**

infant;
child;
son

This character for child originated from a representation of an infant with outstretched arms and legs. Eventually it was modified to one with legs swaddled in cloth bands. Evidently, to the Chinese parent, the secret of infant care lies in keeping one end wet and the other end dry.

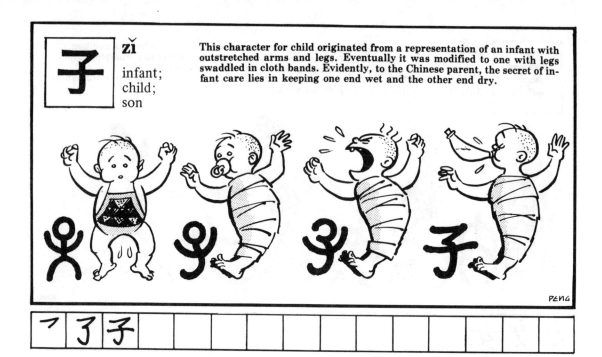

PENG

｀ 了 子

子弹	zǐ dàn	bullet
子弟	zǐ dì	young generations
子女	zǐ nǚ	children
子孙	zǐ sūn	descendants

子夜	zǐ yè	midnight
子音	zǐ yīn	consonant
子子孙孙	zǐ zǐ sūn sūn	descendants
孩子	hái zǐ	child

Example:

这 个 孩 子 很 聪 明 。
Zhè gè hái zǐ hěn cōng míng.

It means, "This child is very intelligent."

2

好 HǍO
good; right; excellent

Man combined 女 (girl or daughter) with 子 (child or son) to form a character for goodness and excellence. From experience he must have found his greatest good in the possession of a wife and a child or a son and a daughter. It is also good that his wife sticks to his child.

ㄑ ㄠ 女 女ˇ 妤 好

好吃	hǎo chī	delicious
好处	hǎo chù	benefit; advantage
好感	hǎo gǎn	good impression
好汉	hǎo hàn	worthy man
好久	hǎo jiǔ	a long time
好看	hǎo kàn	good looking
好听	hǎo tīng	pleasant to the ear
好象	hǎo xiàng	look alike

好笑	hǎo xiào	funny
好心	hǎo xīn	kind-hearted
好意	hǎo yì	well-intentioned
好在	hǎo zài	fortunately; thanks to
好转	hǎo zhuǎn	turn for the better
好人好事	hǎo rén hǎo shì	good personalities and good deeds

Example:

这 首 歌 很 好 听 。
Zhè shǒu gē hěn hǎo tīng.
It means, "This song is very pleasant to the ear."

3

安 ĀN

peace; contentment

The character for peace and contentment is made up of woman (女) and roof (宀). Man conceived the idea that to attain peace he should have only one woman under the roof or confine her within the house.

安定	ān dìng	stable
安静	ān jìng	serene; quiet or peaceful
安乐	ān lè	peace and happiness
安眠	ān mián	sleep peacefully
安宁	ān níng	peaceful; free from troubles
安排	ān pái	arrange
安全	ān quán	safe; secure

安慰	ān wèi	comfort; console
安心	ān xīn	feel at ease; free from worries
安装	ān zhuāng	install; assemble
安分守己	ān fèn shǒu jǐ	law abiding; be contented with one's lot
安居乐业	ān jū lè yè	live and work in contentment
不安	bù ān	uneasy; worried

Example:

用 行 人 天 桥 过 路 最 安 全 。
Yòng xíng rén tiān qiáo 'guò lù zuì ān quán.

It means, "The safest way to cross the road is to use an overhead bridge."

4

字 **zì**

written character

To preserve written characters from deterioration man transcribed them on bamboo bound into books. Such precious written words came to be cherished as a child (子) is cherished under a roof (宀). Hence 字: the written character.

Pictured here under the roof is a precious youthful character being preserved from deterioration.

宁

丶 丷 宀 宁 字 字

字典	zì diǎn	dictionary
字号	zì hào	name of shop
字迹	zì jì	handwriting
字据	zì jù	written receipt
字句	zì jù	words and expressions

字母	zì mǔ	letter of an alphabet
字幕	zì mù	subtitle
字体	zì tǐ	style of calligraphy
字里行间	zì lǐ háng jiān	between the lines
写字	xiě zì	writing (words)

Example:

他 的 字 体 很 美 。
Tā de zì tǐ hěn měi.

It means, "His handwriting is very beautiful."

豕 **shǐ**
pig

In this pictograph of pig the head is replaced by a line (一). On the left are the belly and paws (豸) and on the right the back and tail (乀). The domestic pig might well symbolise prosperity to man, so closely knit and tied together were their lives. This interdependence probably gave rise to the proverbial saying: "The schoolmaster should not leave his books, nor the poor man his pig."

一	丆	丁	豕	豕	豕	豕						

豕 (shǐ) is the literary term for pig and is practically obsolete. 猪 (zhū) is being used instead.

猪排	zhū pái	pork ribs
猪肉	zhū ròu	pork
猪油	zhū yóu	lard
猪肝色	zhū gān sè	maroon colour
懒猪	lǎn zhū	lazy pig

Example:

回 教 徒 不 能 吃 猪 肉 。
Huí jiào tú bù néng chī zhū ròu.

It means, "Muslims cannot eat pork."

6

家

jiā

house; family

A pig (豕) under the roof (宀) gave man his concept of home (家). Domesticated, the pig brought man no domestic trouble and was allowed freedom to wander about in the house.

` ` 宀 宀 宀 宁 宋 家 家 家

家产	jiā chǎn	family's property
家畜	jiā chù	domestic animals; livestock
家具	jiā jù	furniture
家眷	jiā juàn	family (wife and children)
家庭	jiā tíng	family; home
家务	jiā wù	household chores
家乡	jiā xiāng	native place

家园	jiā yuán	native place; homeland
家长	jiā zhǎng	parents
家政	jiā zhèng	domestic science; domestic affairs
家族	jiā zú	clan or the family
家常便饭	jiā cháng biàn fàn	ordinary meal
家家户户	jiā jiā hù hù	every family
家破人亡	jiā pò rén wáng	broken family and its members demised
家喻户晓	jiā yù hù xiǎo	known to every household

Example:

我 有 一 个 快 乐 的 家 庭 。

Wǒ yǒu yī gè kuài lè de jiā tíng.

It means, "I have a happy family."

嫁 **jià**
to marry
a man

This character, derived by adding home (家) to woman (女), provides an incentive for a girl to marry. It applies only to woman who, in marriage, adds to her possessions a husband, a home and a family.

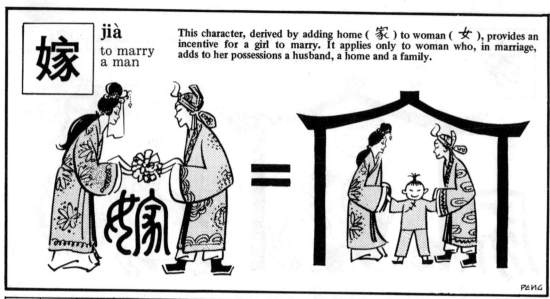

く	女	女	女	女	女	女	妒	妒	嫁	嫁	嫁	

嫁娶	jià qǔ	marriage	
嫁人	jià rén	get married	
嫁妆	jià zhuāng	trousseau	

嫁祸于人	jià huò yú rén	put blame on others
出嫁	chū jià	be married

Example:

自 己 做 错 事 要 承 认 ， 不 要 嫁 祸 于 人 。
Zì jǐ zuò cuò shì yào chéng rèn, bù yào jià huò yú rén.

It means, "One should admit one's mistakes and not put the blame on others."

8

妻　**qī**　wife

When man marries woman he puts a broom ψ into her hand ヨ bestowing upon her the rulership of the house. Hence 妻 : a wife — one who wields the broom, using it to take care of house and home.

一　コ　ヨ　ヨ　事　妻　妻　妻

妻舅	qī jiù	brother-in-law
妻室	qī shì	legal wife
妻子	qī zi	wife

妻离子散	qī lí zǐ sàn	broken up family
贤妻	xián qī	good wife

Example:

他 有 一 个 美 丽 的 妻 子 。

Tā yǒu yī gè měi lì de qī zi.

It means, "He has a pretty wife."

9

木　**mù**
tree;
wood

This is a pictograph of a tree
with its branches (一), trunk (丨)
and roots (八). Only the trunk
and branches are suggested
because 木 also stands for wood.
The 木 pictured here didn't
stand very long though.

一 十 才 木

木板	mù bǎn	wooden plank or board
木材	mù cái	timber
木筏	mù fá	wooden raft
木工	mù gōng	carpentry
木瓜	mù guā	papaya
木屐	mù jī	clogs
木匠	mù jiàng	carpenter
木刻	mù kè	wood carving
木料	mù liào	timber; lumber

木偶戏	mù'ǒu xì	puppet show
木炭	mù tàn	charcoal
木头	mù tóu	wooden block; wood
木星	Mù Xīng	Jupiter
木乃伊	mù nǎi yī	mummy
木已成舟	mù yǐ chéng zhōu	(wood has become a boat) What's done cannot be undone
麻木	má mù	numb

Example:

小 英 喜 欢 看 木 偶 戏 。
Xiǎo Yīng xǐ huān kàn mù'ǒu xì.
It means, "Xiao Ying likes to watch puppet shows."

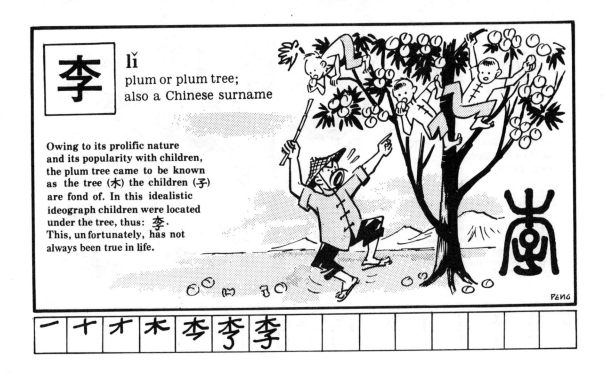

李

lǐ

plum or plum tree;
also a Chinese surname

Owing to its prolific nature
and its popularity with children,
the plum tree came to be known
as the tree (木) the children (子)
are fond of. In this idealistic
ideograph children were located
under the tree, thus: 李.
This, unfortunately, has not
always been true in life.

一 十 才 木 李 李 李

李树	lǐ shù	plum tree
李子	lǐ zi	plum
行李	xíng li	baggage; luggage
行李箱	xíng lǐ xiāng	trunk

Example:

去 旅 行 ， 最 好 不 要 带 太 多 行 李 。

Qù lǚ xíng, zuì hǎo bù yào dài tài duō xíng li.

It means, "When travelling, it is advisable not to bring along too many baggage."

11

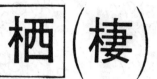

qī

to roost, perch or nest;
to live in poverty or
seek refuge

This character is built on tree (木)
as radical and wife (妻) as phonetic.
The tree provides the base and
the wife supplies the sound.
Man simplified it by putting
西 in place of wife, the character
for "west" (西).

| 一 | 十 | 才 | 木 | 朳 | 朽 | 栖 | 栖 | 栖 | 栖 | | | | | |

栖身	qī shēn	dwell; obtain shelter	栖息	qī xī	rest
栖宿	qī sù	rest for the night	栖身之所	qī shēn zhī suǒ	dwelling-place
			两栖动物	liǎng qī dòng wù	amphibians

Example:

新 加 坡 并 不 乏 栖 身 之 所 。
Xīn Jiā Pō bīng bù quē qī shēn zhī suǒ.
It means, "Singapore does not lack dwelling places."

人 rén

man;
person;
human

The pictographic profile of a person (人) presents an insight into his evolutionary development. Created from earth and equipped with hands and feet, lowly man eked out an existence from the ground with his hands 彐 to help him stand on his feet 礻. Discarding both hands and feet, he used only his head 𠆢. Today, in the race of the survival of the fittest, he loses his head completely 𠆢 and finds himself barely able to keep his feet.

| 丿 | 人 | | | | | | | | | | | |

人才	rén cái	men of talent		人生	rén shēng	the life of man
人格	rén gé	personality		人为	rén wéi	man-made
人工	rén gōng	artificial; man-made		人物	rén wù	personage; notable figure
人口	rén kǒu	population				
人类	rén lèi	mankind		人行道	rén xíng dào	pavement; side-walk
人们	rén mén	general term for a number of people; men		人山人海	rén shān rén hǎi	huge crowds of people
人民	rén mín	people		行人	xíng rén	pedestrian

Example:

在 裕 廊 飞 禽 公 园 有 一 个 人 工 瀑 布 。

Zài Yù Láng fēi qín gōng yuán yǒu yī gè rén gōng pù bù

It means, "There is a man-made waterfall in Jurong Bird Park."

13

大 dà

big; great

The ideographic representation for "big" is simply a front elevation of a full-grown man with arms stretched out to the limit 大. What conveys the idea of "big" is not the size of the man but his demonstrative gesture. Some of the assortment of characters pictured below are trying to show what "big" means. Others are merely trying to show off.

一 ナ 大

大胆	dà dǎn	daring; bold
大概	dà gài	probably
大家	dà jiā	all (people)
大批	dà pī	in great numbers
大人	dà rén	adult
大声	dà shēng	loud voice
大厦	dà shà	big building
大事	dà shì	important matter
大学	dà xuè	university

大选	dà xuǎn	general election
大约	dà yuē	about
大使馆	dà shǐ guǎn	embassy
大众化	dà zhòng huà	popularized
大自然	dà zì rán	the world of nature
大快人心	dà kuài rén xīn	to the satisfaction of the masses
大同小异	dà tóng xiǎo yì	very much the same

Example:

小 英 很 自 大 ， 所 以 人 人 都 讨 厌 她 。
Xiǎo Yīng hěn zì dà, suǒ yǐ rén rén dōu tǎo yàn tā.

It means, "Xiao Ying is very conceited, so everyone dislikes her."

14

天 tiān

**heaven;
sky;
day**

This stylised representation shows man's ability to stand on his feet (人), extending his arms egotistically (大). But high above man (人), be he ever so great (大), stretches the heavenly firmament (一), filling the empty space above his shoulders and directing his footsteps. Hence: 天 , meaning heaven — man's rightful and authoritative head. Since the growing light of the sky ushers in the dawn of day, 天 came to mean also "day".

PENG

| 一 | 二 | 手 | 天 | | | | | | | | | | | |

天才	tiān cái	genius	天真	tiān zhēn	naive; innocent
天空	tiān kōng	sky	天资	tiān zī	natural endowment
天亮	tiān liàng	daylight; day-break	天主教	tiān zhǔ jiào	Roman Catholic
天桥	tiān qiáo	overpass (over-head bridge)	天南地北	tiān nán dì běi	far apart
天然	tiān· rán	natural (not artificial)	白天	bái tiān	daytime
			明天	míng tiān	tomorrow
天生	tiān shēng	inborn	前天	qián tiān	day before yesterday
天下	tiān xià	the whole world	昨天	zuó tiān	yesterday

Example:

明 天 我 要 去 日 本 。
Míng tiān wǒ yào qù Rì Běn .
It means, "I am going to Japan tomorrow."

15

fū

husband;
distinguished
person

A youthful person (人), grown big
(大) and attaining maturity at 20,
used a hairpin (一) and was vested
with the virile cap of manhood 夫 .
Given an honourable name, he was
considered a distinguished person,
qualified as a prospective husband.
Hence 夫 means a distinguished
person or husband.

| 一 | 二 | 𡗜 | 夫 | | | | | | | | | | | |

农夫	nóng fū	farmer		夫妇	fū fù	husband and wife
懦夫	nuò fū	coward		夫妻	fū qī	husband and wife
渔夫	yú fū	fisherman		夫人	fū rén	wife; madam
丈夫	zhàng fu	husband		大夫	dài fū	medical doctor

Example:

小 兰 的 丈 夫 是 个 农 夫 。

Xiǎo-lán de zhàng fu shì gè nóng fū.

It means, "Xiao-lan's husband is a farmer."

tài

too;
over;
excessive

By underscoring "big" (大) with a line (一) man came up with a superlative character (太) meaning too much or over the limit. In the ecstasy of double happiness and the rapture of material bliss that followed, man bestowed upon his wife a flattering title: 太太 a double emphasis. She lived up to it. Man thereafter reduced the underline to a teeny-weeny stroke 太 .

一 ナ 大 太

太多	tài duō	too many
太后	tài hòu	empress dowager
太监	tài jiàn	eunuch
太空	tài kōng	outer space; sky
太平	tài píng	peace
太太	tài tài	madam
太阳	tài yáng	sun
太子	tài zǐ	prince

太极拳	tài jí quán	kind of traditional Chinese martial art
太空船	tài kōng chuán	spaceship
太空人	tài kōng rén	spaceman
太平门	tài píng mén	emergency exit; safety exit
太平洋	Tài Píng Yáng	Pacific Ocean
太阳能	tài yáng néng	solar energy

Example:

太 空 人 已 在 月 球 登 陆 。
Tài kōng rén yǐ zài yuè qiú dēng lù.
It means, "The spaceman has already landed on the moon."

立 lì — stand; rise up

This character, meaning plain standing or rising up, portrays a person standing — not in the abstract, but on firm, stable ground (一). Originally written 𡗶, it was modified to 企 and finally to 立. Illustrated here are some human characters, firm and infirm, trying to stand on stable ground and demonstrating that plain standing is not plain sailing.

PENG

丶 亠 六 立 立

立场	lì chǎng	standpoint; position	
立法	lì fǎ	legislation	
立功	lì gōng	perform meritorious service	
立即	lì jí	at once; immediately	
立刻	lì kè	immediately; instantly	
立体	lì tǐ	three-dimensional	

立约	lì yuē	enter into an agreement
立正	lì zhèng	attention! (army command)
立志	lì zhì	be determined (to do something)
立足	lì zú	base oneself on
建立	jiàn lì	establish; erect
设立	shè lì	set up; establish

Example:

我 们 在 花 园 里 建 立 起 一 座 纪 念 碑 。
Wǒ mén zài huā yuán lǐ jiàn lì qǐ yī zuò jì niàn bēi.
It means, "We have erected a monument in the garden."

18

xiǎo

小

small;
petty;
young

A vertical stroke, (亅),
separating two little ones
(八) gave man his concept of
"small". The idea was also
derived from the division (八) of
an object (亅) already small by
its nature. To man, division (÷)
makes small (小) and
multiplication (✕) makes big
(大) a thing. Our illustration
shows how to multiply happiness
by dividing sorrow.

小
small

大
big

PENG

亅	小	小										

小吃	xiǎo chī	snacks
小丑	xiǎo chǒu	clown
小岛	xiǎo dǎo	small island; islet
小姐	xiǎo jiě	lady; Miss
小麦	xiǎo mài	wheat
小声	xiǎo shēng	low voice; whisper
小时	xiǎo shí	hour

小偷	xiǎo tōu	thief
小心	xiǎo xīn	careful; cautious
小型	xiǎo xíng	small scale
小学	xiǎo xué	primary school
小组	xiǎo zǔ	small team or group
小题大作	xiǎo tí dà zuò	make a mountain out of a molehill

Example:

我 喜 欢 巴 金 的 小 说 。
Wǒ xǐ huān Bā-jīn de xiǎo shuō.
It means, "I like Ba Jin's novels."

少 shǎo

less; few; short of

This character combines 小 with ノ to form 少. It means to cut smaller or diminish (ノ) that which is already small (小), thus making it less (少). To cut short the diminishing process, the method suggested below is an effective short cut to reduce big (大) to small (小) and small (小) to less (少).

ノ	小	小	少

少妇	shào fù	young married woman
少量	shǎo liàng	small quantity
少年	shào nián	teenager; youngster
少女	shào nǚ	young girl
少数	shǎo shù	minority
少许	shǎo xǔ	little; few
少有	shǎo yǒu	rare; scarce;

少壮	shào zhuàng	youthful and strong
少不了	shǎo bù liǎo	indispensable
少见多怪	shǎo jiàn duō guài	things appear strange to the unfamiliar
少数民族	shǎo shù mín zú	ethnic minority
多少	duō shǎo	how many; how much

Example:

这 位 少 女 真 美 丽 。
Zhè wèi shào nǚ zhēn měi lì.

It means, "This young lady is beautiful indeed."

20

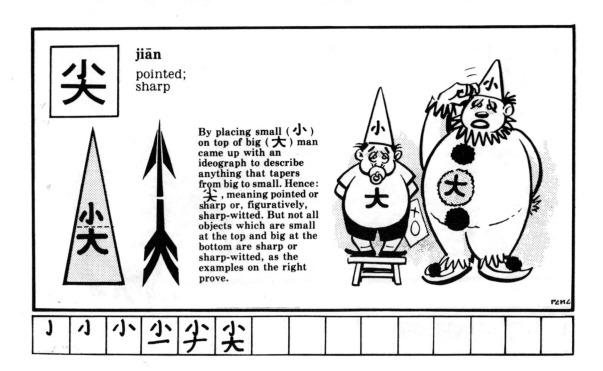

jiān

pointed;
sharp

By placing small (小) on top of big (大) man came up with an ideograph to describe anything that tapers from big to small. Hence: 尖, meaning pointed or sharp or, figuratively, sharp-witted. But not all objects which are small at the top and big at the bottom are sharp or sharp-witted, as the examples on the right prove.

尖兵	jiān bīng	vanguard
尖刀	jiān dāo	sharp knife
尖顶	jiān dǐng	peak; apex
尖端	jiān duān	highest point

尖刻	jiān kè	trenchant (of words; speech)
尖利	jiān lì	sharp
尖锐	jiān ruì	sharp; pointed
尖塔	jiān tǎ	spire

Example:

这 是 一 把 尖 锐 的 刀 。
Zhè shì yī bǎ jiān ruì de dāo.
It means, "This is a sharp knife."

21

tián

田

rice field;
grain field

From dawn to dusk man toiled in the field, taking to heart the proverbial saying: "Never leave your field in spring or your house in winter." The character he shaped for "field" was a pictograph of a ploughed field with furrows and cross-paths: 田 . By the sweat of his brow he reaped the fruits of his labour. But all that toil has left its mark of furrows and cross-paths, not only on the field, but also indelibly on his brow.

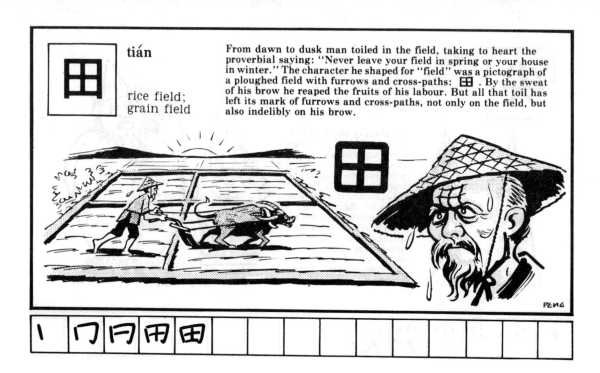

丶 冂 冂 田 田

田地	tián dì	field or situation (of something)	田园	tián yuán	fields and gardens
田鸡	tián jī	frog	田径赛	tián jìng sài	athletic competition
田径	tián jìng	track and field	耕田	gēng tián	plough
田野	tián yě	open country			

Example:

一 年 一 度 的 田 径 赛 又 将 来 临 了 。

Yī nián yī dù de tián jìng sài yòu jiāng lái lín le.

It means, "The annual athletic competition is round the corner again."

22

力 **lì**
strength;
force;
power

In the original form (扬) the long middle line (᠊), curved at the top to take less room, represents the sinew that binds muscle to bone. The other line (𝖭) pictures the fibrous sheath of the sinew.

The modern version (力) is a powerful graphic impression of the forearm — a symbol of physical strength. Moral strength, however, is more to be desired. And those who go by the rule: "Might is right" will soon have to learn that "Right is might".

PENG

| 乛 | 力 | | | | | | | | | | | | | |

力量	lì liang	physical strength; force	
力气	lì qì	effort; strength	
力求	lì qiú	strive; make every effort	
力争	lì zhēng	endeavour; fight for	

力不从心	lì bù cóng xīn	ability falling short of one's wishes
力求进步	lì qiú jìn bù	struggle for improvement
力争上游	lì zhēng shàng yóu	aim high
人力	rén lì	labour force; manpower

Example:

团 结 就 是 力 量 。
Tuán jié jiù shì lì liang.
It means, "Unity is strength."

23

男

nán

man;
male;
masculine

A field (田), where strength (力) is exerted, is the symbol for "masculine" man 男, the male of the human species. This is probably because the home is where the female of the same species exerts her strength. Our picture shows strength being exerted — by the male (男) in field-work, the female (女) in housework, and their offspring (子) in promotional work.

| 丶 | 冂 | 冂 | 甪 | 田 | 罗 | 男 | | | | | | | |

男孩	nán hái	boy	男子	nán zǐ	man; male
男女	nán nǚ	men and women	男朋友	nán péng yǒu	boy friend
男人	nán rén	man	男子汉	nán zǐ hàn	man; hero
男声	nán shēng	male voice	男男女女	nán nán nǚ nǚ	men and women
男性	nán xìng	male	男女平等	nán nǚ píng děng	equality of men and women
男装	nán zhuāng	male attire			

Example:

很 多 好 厨 师 都 是 男 性 。
Hěn duō hǎo chú shī dōu shì nán xìng.
It means, "Many good chefs are males."

日　**rì**　sun; day

The sun was first depicted as a circle with an "eye" or centre and rays extending to the corners of the earth ✳. This was simplified to ⊙, then modified: ⊖, and finally squared off: 日. Just as surely as its rising and setting mark the "day" (日) for man, the sun's shining upon the wicked as well as the good demonstrates that it sees the whole world with one eye.

一	冂	月	日												

日报	rì bào	daily newspaper	日薪	rì xīn	daily wages
日本	Rì Běn	Japan	日夜	rì yè	day and night
日常	rì cháng	daily; usual	日子	rì zǐ	day; life
日出	rì chū	sunrise	日光浴	rì guāng yù	sun bath
日光	rì guāng	sunshine	日内瓦	Rì Nèi Wǎ	Geneva
日记	rì jì	diary	日用品	rì yòng pǐn	daily necessities
日历	rì lì	calendar	日常生活	rì cháng shēng huó	daily life
日期	rì qī	date	日以继夜	rì yǐ jì yè	day and night; non-stop
日蚀	rì shí (shi)	eclipse of the sun			

Example:

我 明 天 要 上 山 顶 看 日 出 。
Wǒ míng tiān yào shàng shān dǐng kàn rì chū.

It means, "I'm going to the hilltop tomorrow to watch sunrise."

25

月 yuè

moon;
month

To form the character for moon (or lunar month) man chose the crescent 〗. The original pictograph suggested two phases of a waxing new moon 〗. Tilting it: 〗 and then directing it earthwards: 〗 exposed man to the influence of moonbeam radiation — with striking consequences. Pictured here is a beaming moon casting its spell on some beaming moonstruck earthlings.

| | | | | | | | | | | | |
|丿|几|月|月| | | | | | | | |

月饼	yuè bǐng	mooncake	
月份	yuè fèn	month	
月光	yuè guāng	moonlight	
月经	yuè jīng	menstruation	
月刊	yuè kān	monthly publication	
月亮	yuè liang	moon	
月票	yuè piào	monthly ticket	
月球	yuè qiú	the moon	

月色	yuè sè	moonlight
月蚀	yuè shí (shi)	eclipse of the moon
月薪	yuè xīn	monthly salary
月夜	yuè yè	moonlit night
月下老人	yuè xià lǎo rén	matchmaker
赏月	shǎng yuè	enjoy the moonlight

Example:

我 们 一 面 赏 月 ， 一 面 吃 月 饼 。
Wǒ mén yī miàn shǎng yuè, yī miàn chī yuè bǐng.

It means, "We ate mooncakes while enjoying the moonlight."

26

明 míng

brilliant;
bright;
enlightened

Man combined the sun (日) and the moon (月) to produce an ideograph for bright, brilliant or enlightened. He called it: "ming" (明) and used it also for the brilliant Ming Dynasty of China which came in the wake of the Dark Ages of Europe. Today science and technology has ushered in the dazzling Space Age — with man very much enlightened and the future very much bedarkened.

PENG

| 一 | 冂 | 月 | 日 | 日刀 | 明 | 明 | 明 | | | | | |

明白	míng bái	understand; clear
明亮	míng liàng	shining; bright
明朗	míng lǎng	bright and clear
明媚	míng mèi	bright and beautiful
明年	míng nián	next year
明显	míng xiǎn	obvious
明智	míng zhì	wise
明晃晃	míng huǎng huǎng	glaring; shining
明信片	míng xìn piàn	postcard

明辨是非	míng biàn shì fēi	distinguish right from wrong
明目张胆	míng mù zhāng dǎn	openly; blatantly
明争暗斗	míng zhēng àn dòu	struggle overtly and covertly
明知故犯	míng zhī gù fàn	commit mistakes deliberately
明知故问	míng zhī gù wèn	question knowingly

Example:

我 明 白 你 的 意 思 。
Wǒ míng bái nǐ de yì sī.

It means, "I understand what you mean."

bái

白

clear;
white;
plain

As the sun (日) peeps above the horizon its very first ray (′) begins to dispel the shadowy haze of night. Hence, 白 , the symbol for clear, white or plain. Man easily understands anything that is bright (明) and clear (白), so "bright and clear" means to understand (明 白). Apparently, this is not always easily understood as our picture shows.

白菜	bái cài	Chinese cabbage	白茫茫	bai máng máng	an endless whiteness
白费	bái fèi	in vain; waste			
白宫	Bái Gōng	The White House (official residence of the president of America)	白日梦	bái rì mèng	daydream
			白血球	bái xuè qiú	white corpuscle
			白手起家	bái shǒu qǐ jiā	start from scratch; build up from nothing
白喉	bái hóu	diphtheria			
白色	bái sè	white colour	坦白	tǎn bái	frank
白糖	bái táng	white sugar	真象大白	zhēn xiàng dà bái	matter that is finally made clear
白兔	bái tù	white rabbit			

Example:

他 对 我 很 坦 白 。
Tā duì wǒ hěn tǎn bái.

It means, "He is very frank to me."

28

旦 dàn

dawn; daybreak

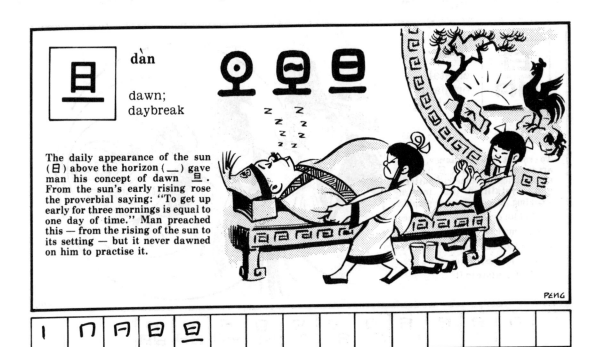

The daily appearance of the sun (日) above the horizon (一) gave man his concept of dawn 旦. From the sun's early rising rose the proverbial saying: "To get up early for three mornings is equal to one day of time." Man preached this — from the rising of the sun to its setting — but it never dawned on him to practise it.

丨	冂	日	日	旦						

旦暮	dàn mù	morning and evening	花旦	huā dàn	prima dona in an opera
旦夕	dàn xī	in a short while	元旦	yuán dàn	New Year's Day
旦夕之间	dàn xī zhī jiān	within a single day	一旦	yī dàn	once; as soon as

Example:

元 旦 是 公 共 假 期 。

Yúan dàn shì gōng gòng jià qī.

It means, "New Year's Day is a public holiday."

29

jīng

crystal;
brilliant;
sparkling

To reflect his brilliance, man arranged three suns (日) into a symmetrical, geometric pattern and crystallized this into a sparkling ideograph and graphic symbol for crystal: 晶. For generations man has been gazing into his crystal ball but, crystal-clear though it was, he couldn't see much of a future in it.

PENG

晶体	jīng tǐ	crystal	亮晶晶	liàng jīng·jīng	shining
晶莹	jīng yíng	lustrous; brilliant	水晶	shuǐ jīng	crystalline
晶体管	jīng tǐ guǎn	transistor			
结晶	jié jīng	result; product; crystallization			

Example:

这 本 书 是 他 多 年 研 究 的 结 晶 。

Zhè běn shū shì tā duō nián yán jiū de jié jīng.

It means, "This book is the result of his many years of research."

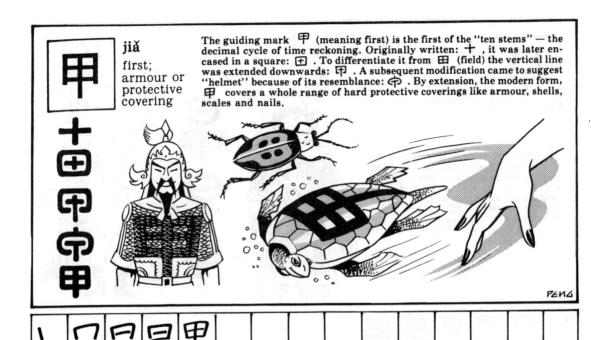

jiǎ

first; armour or protective covering

The guiding mark 甲 (meaning first) is the first of the "ten stems" — the decimal cycle of time reckoning. Originally written: 十 , it was later encased in a square: 田 . To differentiate it from 田 (field) the vertical line was extended downwards: 甲 . A subsequent modification came to suggest "helmet" because of its resemblance: 甲 . By extension, the modern form, 甲 covers a whole range of hard protective coverings like armour, shells, scales and nails.

甲板	jiǎ bǎn	deck of a ship
甲虫	jiǎ chóng	beetle
甲等	jiǎ děng	first class or first grade
甲克	jiǎ kè	jacket
甲壳	jiǎ qiào	crust

甲鱼	jiǎ yú	soft-shelled turtle
甲骨文	jiǎ gǔ wén	inscriptions on oracle bones
甲状腺	jiǎ zhuàng xiàn	thyroid gland
装甲兵	zhuāng jiǎ bīng	armoured corps

Example:

有 许 多 人 在 甲 板 上 作 日 光 浴 。
Yǒu xǔ duō rén zài jiǎn bǎn shàng zuò rì guāng yù.

It means, "There are many people sunbathing on the deck."

zǎo

early;
morning

早 (meaning early or morning) is the time of the day when the sun (日) has risen to the height of a man's helmet (十). 十 is the old form of 甲, originally meaning helmet. Since another meaning of 甲 (十) is "first", the character: 早 signifies also the first (十) sun (日), that is, the early morning: 早 .

丨	冂	曰	日	旦	早									

早安	zǎo ān	good morning		早年	zǎo nián	one's early life
早班	zǎo bān	morning shift		早期	zǎo qī	early stage
早餐	zǎo cān	breakfast		早日	zǎo rì	at an early date
早操	zǎo cāo	morning exercise		早上	zǎo shàng	(early) morning
早晨	zǎo chén	early morning		早晚	zǎo wǎn	morning and evening
早春	zǎo chūn	early spring				
早婚	zǎo hūn	marrying too early				

Example:

请 早 日 答 覆 。

Qǐng zǎo rì dá fù.

It means, "Please reply as soon as possible."

休 xiū

rest; cease

This is a refreshing character for any person (人) working near a shady tree (木). It literally means "rest" (休) and pictures a person (人 or 亻) leaning against a tree (木). Of the tree the Chinese proverb laments: "One generation plants the trees under whose shade another generation takes its ease." Exemplifying this, we show a character leisurely basking in the sunshine and leaning himself against a tree planted by an older generation.

ノ 亻 仁 什 休 休

休会	xiū huì	adjourn (meeting)
休假	xiū jià	on leave
休息	xiū xi	rest or relax
休闲	xiū xián	lie fallow (land)
休想	xiū xiǎng	don't expect
休学	xiū xué	suspend one's schooling without losing one's status as a student
休养	xiū yǎng	recuperate or convalesce
休业	xiū yè	wind up (business)
休战	xiū zhàn	ceasefire
休整	xiū zhěng	rest and reorganize
休止	xiū zhǐ	cease or stop

Example:

他 在 医 院 里 休 养 。

Tā zài yī yuàn lǐ xiū yǎng.

It means, "He is recuperating in the hospital."

33

东（東） dōng

east

Man turned his head around, looking for a suitable sign for "east" — the direction he faced when he saw the sun rise every day. He succeeded one morning when he observed the sun (日) through the trees (木). So sun (日) behind tree (木) became east (東). Fortunately, success did not turn man's head, otherwise he would have been left facing the wrong direction.

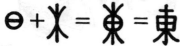

一 七 车 车 东

东方	dōng fāng	the East
东风	dōng fēng	east wind
东京	Dōng Jīng	Tokyo
东欧	Dōng Ōu	Eastern Europe
东西	dōng xī	things; East and West
东半球	dōng bàn qiú	eastern hemisphere
东方人	Dōng Fāng Rén	Orientals

东南亚	Dōng Nán Yà	Southeast Asia
东奔西走	dōng bēn xī zǒu	busy oneself with
东山再起	dōng shān zài qǐ	stage a come-back
东西南北	Dōng Xī Nán Běi	East, West, South, North
东张西望	dōng zhāng xī wàng	gaze (or peer) around

Example:

太 阳 由 东 方 升 上 来 。

Tài yáng yóu dōng fāng shēng shàng lái .

It means, "The sun rises in the east."

西 **xī**

west

As the sun settles in the west birds roost in their nests; so a cross-hatched bird's nest provided the cradle for "west", and nest became west. Man's fertile imagination conceived a new ideograph — a nest with a brooding bird: hatching up a new form: 西 which finally developed into a full-fledged character for west: 西. As all "things" exist between east (東) and west (西), the combination east-west, meaning "things", came to be applied to anything from east to west.

PENG

一 厂 厅 丙 両 西

西边	xī biɑn	west side
西餐	xī cān	Western-style food
西方	xī fāng	the West
西瓜	xī guā	watermelon
西湖	Xī Hú	West Lake in Hangzhou
西南	xī nán	southwest
西欧	Xī Ōu	Western Europe

西洋	Xī Yáng	the West
西医	xī yī	a doctor trained in Western medicine
西藏	Xī Zàng	Tibet
西装	xī zhuāng	Western dress
西半球	xī bàn qiú	western hemisphere
西班牙	Xī Bān Yá	Spain
西伯利亚	Xī Bó Lì Yà	Siberia

Example:

西 瓜 有 许 多 种 子 。
Xī quā yǒu xǔ duō zhǒng zi.

It means, "A watermelon has many seeds."

35

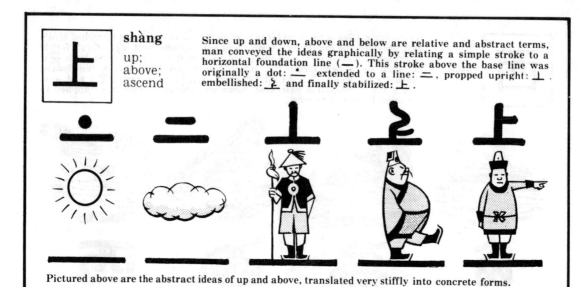

shàng

up;
above;
ascend

Since up and down, above and below are relative and abstract terms, man conveyed the ideas graphically by relating a simple stroke to a horizontal foundation line (—). This stroke above the base line was originally a dot: ∸ extended to a line: ⸗ , propped upright: ⊥ , embellished: ≵ and finally stabilized: 上 .

Pictured above are the abstract ideas of up and above, translated very stiffly into concrete forms.

| 一 | 卜 | 上 | | | | | | | | | | | | | |

上班	shàng bān	go to work	上代	shàng dài	former generations
上辈	shàng bèi	one's elders	上当	shàng dàng	cheated
上宾	shàng bīn	distinguished guest; guest of honour	上等	shàng děng	first-class
			上帝	shàng dì	God
上苍	shàng cāng	Heaven; God	上级	shàng jí	higher authority
上策	shàng cè	the best plan	上课	shàng kè	attend class
上层	shàng céng	upper strata	上空	shàng kōng	in the sky; overhead
上场	shàng chǎng	appear on the stage			
上床	shàng chuáng	go to bed	上游	shàng yóu	upper stream

Example:

她 上 班 去 了 。

Tā shàng bān qù le.

It means, "She's gone to work."

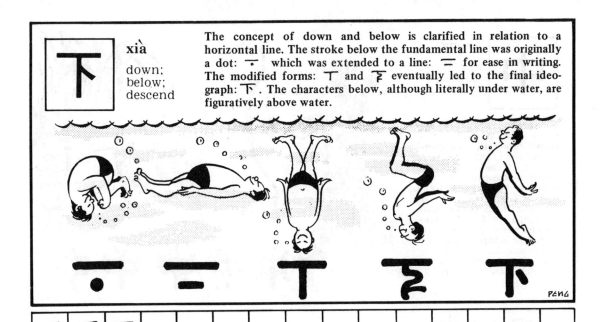

下 xià
down;
below;
descend

The concept of down and below is clarified in relation to a horizontal line. The stroke below the fundamental line was originally a dot: � which was extended to a line: � for ease in writing. The modified forms: 丁 and 下 eventually led to the final ideograph: 下. The characters below, although literally under water, are figuratively above water.

一	丁	下											

下班	xià bān	be off duty	下级	xià jí	lower level
下辈	xià bèi	the younger generation of a family	下贱	xià jiàn	mean; degrading
			下降	xià jiàng	descend
下策	xià cè	bad plan	下课	xià kè	class is over
下层	xià céng	lower level	下来	xià lai	come down
下场	xià chǎng	end; fate	下令	xià lìng	instruct; order
下沉	xià chén	sink	下流	xià liú	despicable
下等	xià děng	low grade	下落	xià luò	whereabouts

Example:

他 下 午 要 去 看 戏 。
Tā xià wǔ yào qù kàn xì.
It means, "He is going for a show in the afternoon."

37

zhōng

中

centre;
middle;neutral

By shooting an arrow: | right into the centre of a square target: 口 man scored a bull's-eye and secured a mark for "centre": 中. He added a decoration of four stripes: 中, rearranged them: 中, stripped them off: 中, and finally hit his mark for simplicity: 中. The symbol also means standing in the middle or neutrality (中立). Unfortunately, in the application of neutrality, man has completely missed his mark.

PENG

| 丶 | 冂 | 口 | 中 | | | | | | | | | | | |

中部	zhōng bù	central section		中华	Zhōng Huā	China
中餐	zhōng cān	Chinese meal		中间	zhōng jiān	middle
中层	zhōng céng	middle-level		中立	zhōng lì	neutral
中程	zhōng céng	intermediate range		中年	zhōng nián	middle-aged
中等	zhōng děng	middle-class		中途	zhōng tú	midway
中东	Zhōng Dōng	the Middle East		中文	zhōng wén	Chinese language
中断	zhōng duàn	break off		中学	zhōng xué	secondary school
中国	Zhōng Guó	China				

Example:

他 出 身 中 等 家 庭 。
Tā chū shēn zhōng děng jiā tíng.

It means, "He comes from a middle-class family."

奴 nú

slave; servant

A woman 女 under the hand 又 of a master signifies slave 奴. The components 又 and 女 put together literally mean "handmaid" — a female who slaves with her hands. 奴 includes slaves of both sexes who serve their masters hand and foot.

〈	夊	女	奵	奴									

奴婢	nú bī	female slave
奴才	nú cai	flunkey; lackey
奴化	nú huà	enslave
奴隶	nú lì	slave
奴仆	nú pú	male slave

奴性	nú xìng	servile disposition
奴役	nú yì	slavery
奴隶制度	nú lì zhì dù	slave system

Example:

奴 隶 制 度 已 废 除 。

Nú lì zhì dù yǐ fèi chú.

It means, "Slavery has already been abolished."

39

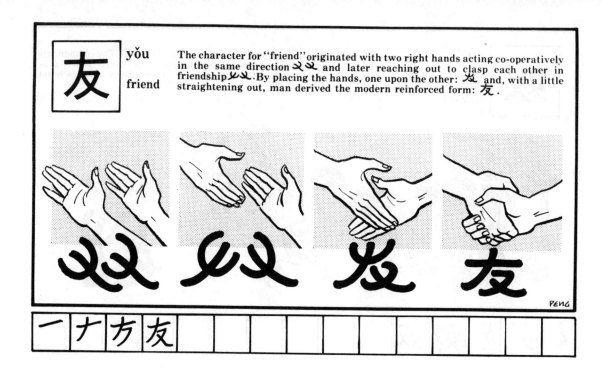

友　yǒu　friend

The character for "friend" originated with two right hands acting co-operatively in the same direction 刄刄 and later reaching out to clasp each other in friendship 刄刄 .By placing the hands, one upon the other: 发 and, with a little straightening out, man derived the modern reinforced form: 友 .

PENG

一　ナ　方　友

友爱	yǒu ài	friendly affection	友人	yǒu rén	friend
友邦	yǒu bāng	friendly nation	友善	yǒu shàn	friendly
友好	yǒu hǎo	friendly	友谊	yǒu yì	friendship
友情	yǒu qíng	friendship	友好协定	yǒu hǎo xié dìng	friendship pact

Example:

他 是 我 的 好 朋 友 。
Tā shì wǒ de hǎo péng yǒu.
It means, "He is my good friend."

40

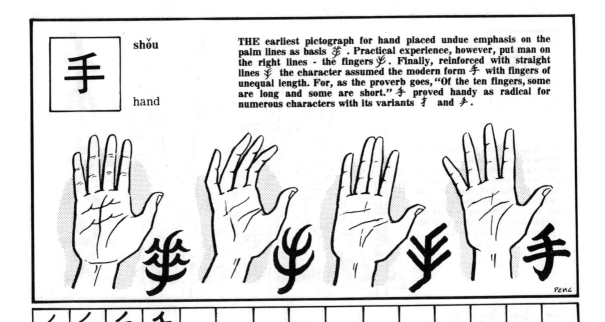

手　shǒu

hand

THE earliest pictograph for hand placed undue emphasis on the palm lines as basis 𝟮 . Practical experience, however, put man on the right lines - the fingers ψ . Finally, reinforced with straight lines ψ the character assumed the modern form 手 with fingers of unequal length. For, as the proverb goes, "Of the ten fingers, some are long and some are short." 手 proved handy as radical for numerous characters with its variants 扌 and 手.

ノ 一 二 手

手臂	shǒu bì	arm
手笔	shǒu bǐ	somebody's own handwriting or painting
手表	shǒu biǎo	wrist-watch
手册	shǒu cè	handbook
手段	shǒu duàn	means; measure
手法	shǒu fǎ	skill; tricks
手工	shǒu gōng	handwork

手巾	shǒu jīn	towel
手铐	shǒu kào	handcuffs
手枪	shǒu qiāng	pistol
手术	shǒu shù	surgical operation
手书	shǒu shū	handwritten letter
手套	shǒu tào	gloves
手电筒	shǒu diàn tǒng	torch
手榴弹	shǒu liú dàn	hand-grenade

Example:

我 有 一 双 手 。
Wǒ yǒu yī shuāng shǒu.

It means, "I have a pair of hands."

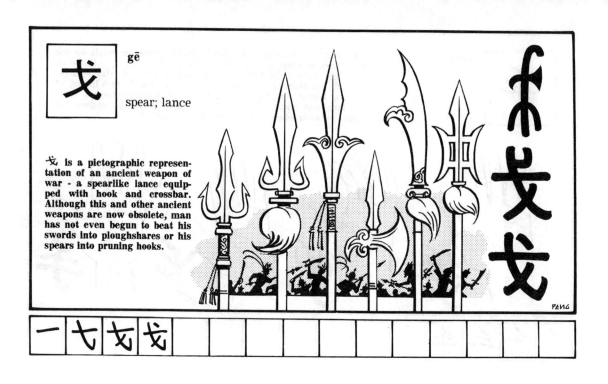

戈 gē

spear; lance

戈 is a pictographic representation of an ancient weapon of war - a spearlike lance equipped with hook and crossbar. Although this and other ancient weapons are now obsolete, man has not even begun to beat his swords into ploughshares or his spears into pruning hooks.

一	弋	戈	戈												

戈壁	Gē bí	the Gobi Desert
干戈	gān gē	weapons; war
倒戈相向	dǎo gē xiāng xiàng	betray one's own party

Example:

化 干 戈 为 玉 帛 。

Huà gān gē wéi yù bó.

It means, "Stop war and make peace."

42

我

wǒ

I; me

THE earliest forms show two spears against each other in direct confrontation: 㦵, presumably symbolizing two rights being asserted and, by extension, my right, that is, me. A later transcription projected a new image: 我, a pictograph of a hand 手 grasping a spear 戈, denoting that when man wields in his hand 手 a spear 戈 his ego, the big "I", emerges. Hence 我: I.

43

| ノ | 一 | 千 | 手 | 扚 | 我 | 我 | | | | | | | |

我们　　　　wǒ men　　　　we
我爱你　　　wǒ ài nǐ　　　I love you
我们的　　　wǒ men de　　our; ours
我行我素　　wǒ xíng wǒ sù　persist in one's
　　　　　　　　　　　　　　old ways

Example:

大 家 你 帮 我 ， 我 帮 你 很 快 就 把 活 儿 干 完 了 。
Dà jiā nǐ bāng wǒ, wǒ bāng nǐ hěn kuài jiù bǎ huó er gàn wán liǎo.
It means, "With each one giving the other a helping hand, they soon got the job done."

你 nǐ — you

THE classical character for "you", an equal, was 爾, a pictograph of a balance 巾 loaded with 爻爻 equally on both sides and topped by a phonetic 尒. 爾 was eventually contracted to 尔. By adding 人 (person) to 尔, man introduced the human element and came up with 你 - a person who carries the same weight: you.

丿 亻 亻 伬 伫 伱 你

你好	nǐ hǎo	how do you do	
你们	nǐ men	you (plural)	
你们的	nǐ men de	your; yours (plural)	
你死我活	nǐ sǐ wǒ huó	life and death struggle	

你追我赶　nǐ zhuī wǒ gǎn　try to overtake each other in friendly emulation

Example:

你 好 吗 ?
Nǐ hǎo mā?
It means, "How do you do?", "how are you?", "hello".

44

也 yě

also;
in addition to

ORIGINALLY the character 也 was a representation of an ancient drinking horn, shaped like a funnel. In addition to his rightful belongings, man also appropriated this drinking vessel. To this day it has remained in his possession - a pictograph specially borrowed for the conjunction "also", joining man to his drinking horn.

乛 纩 也

也罢	yě bà	let it be
也好	yě hǎo	may as well
也行	yě xíng	all right
也许	yě xǔ	perhaps
也有	yě yǒu	also have

Example:

他 也 许 会 来 。
Tā yě xǔ huì lái.

It means, "Perhaps he may come."

| 他 | tā | THE character 他 is drawn from 人 (person) and 也 (also). By extension it means "that person also" and refers to the other person: he or she. |

| 丿 | 亻 | 亻 | 㐅 | 他 | | | | | | | | | | | |

他处	tā chu	elsewhere	他日	tā rì	some other day
他的	tā de	his	他乡	tā xiāng	place far away from home
他们	tā men	they			
他人	tā rén	the other person	他自己	tā zì jǐ	himself

Example:

他 是 一 个 渔 夫 。

Tā shì yī gè yú fū.

It means, "He is a fisherman."

46

目　mù

eye

IN ITS primitive form the eye was pictured naturally with eyelids and pupil ◁▷. When stylized: ⊡ its similarity to ▨ (four) deceived man's eye; so it was stood on end: 目 and finally squared off: 目. It would seem that even with his very own eyes man could not see eye to eye.

MY EYE!

目标	mù biāo	aim	目前	mù qián	at present
目的	mù dì	purpose; aim; goal	目送	mù sòng	watch somebody go
目睹	mù dǔ	witness; see for oneself			
			目下	mù xià	now; at present
目光	mù guāng	sight; vision; view	目不转睛	mù bù zhuǎn jīng	stare
目见	mù jiàn	see for oneself	目瞪口呆	mù dèng kǒu dāi	stunned
目力	mù lì	eyesight	目空一切	mù kōng yī qiè	supercilious
目录	mù lù	contents page or index (of book); catalogue	目中无人	mù zhōng wú rén	look down on others; be overweening

Example:

我　目　前　还　不　想　结　婚　。
Wǒ mù qián hái bù xiǎng jié hūn.

It means, "I don't intend to get married now."

47

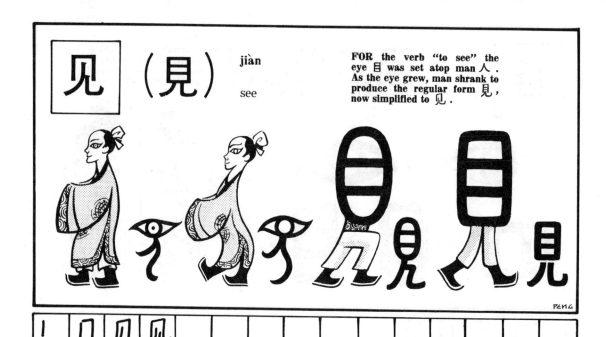

见 （見） jiàn

see

FOR the verb "to see" the eye 目 was set atop man 人. As the eye grew, man shrank to produce the regular form 見, now simplified to 见.

| 丨 | 冂 | 贝 | 见 | | | | | | | | | | | |

见报	jiàn bào	appear in the newspaper
见鬼	jiàn guǐ	preposterous
见解	jiàn jiě	opinions
见谅	jiàn liàng	excuse me; forgive me
见面	jiàn miàn	meet
见识	jiàn shi	widen one's knowledge; enrich one's experience

见闻	jiàn wén	knowledge
见习	jiàn xí	learn on the job
见效	jiàn xiào	effective
见笑	jiàn xiào	laugh at (me or us)
见证	jiàn zhèng	witness; testimony
见异思迁	jiàn yì sī qiān	fickle; inconstant
见义勇为	jiàn yì yǒng wéi	ready to take up the cudgels for a just cause
不见	bù jiàn	lost; disappeared

Example:

我 不 见 了 一 本 书 。
Wǒ bù jiàn le yī běn shū.

It means, "I lost a book."

48

看 kàn

see

IN THIS ideograph man raised his hand 手 above his eye 目 to cut off the sun's rays in order to see clearly 看. From this experience he also saw clearly the point of the Chinese proverb: "You cannot cut off the sunlight with one hand."

ノ ╱ 二 手 乔 乔 看 看 看

看病	kàn bìng	consult a doctor
看穿	kàn chuān	see through
看待	kàn dài	look upon; regard; treat
看到	kàn dào	catch sight of; see
看法	kàn fǎ	view; opinion
看见	kàn jiàn	see
看来	kàn lai	it looks as if
看破	kàn pò	see through

看齐	kàn qí	keep abreast of
看轻	kàn qīng	underestimate
看中	kàn zhòng	take a fancy to
看重	kàn zhòng	think highly of
看不惯	kàn bu guàn	cannot bear the sight of
看得起	kàn de qǐ	think highly of
另眼相看	lìng yǎn xiāng kàn	treated favourably

Example:

他 是 来 看 病 的 。
Tā shì lái kàn bìng de.

It means, "He comes to consult a doctor."

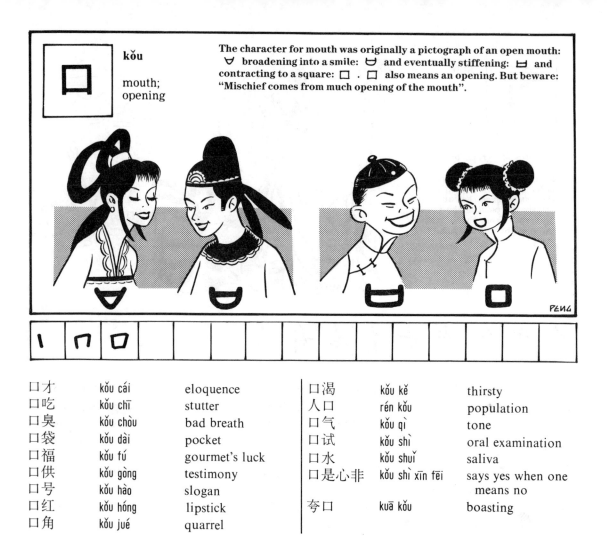

口 **kǒu** mouth; opening

The character for mouth was originally a pictograph of an open mouth: broadening into a smile: and eventually stiffening: and contracting to a square: 口 . 口 also means an opening. But beware: "Mischief comes from much opening of the mouth".

口才	kǒu cái	eloquence	口渴	kǒu kě	thirsty
口吃	kǒu chī	stutter	人口	rén kǒu	population
口臭	kǒu chòu	bad breath	口气	kǒu qì	tone
口袋	kǒu dài	pocket	口试	kǒu shì	oral examination
口福	kǒu fú	gourmet's luck	口水	kǒu shuǐ	saliva
口供	kǒu gòng	testimony	口是心非	kǒu shì xīn fēi	says yes when one means no
口号	kǒu hào	slogan			
口红	kǒu hóng	lipstick	夸口	kuā kǒu	boasting
口角	kǒu jué	quarrel			

Example:

他 的 口 才 很 好 。
Tā de kǒu cái hěn hǎo.

It means, "He is very eloquent."

言

yán

words; speak

"In a multitude of words," the Chinese saying goes, "there will certainly be a mistake." This is evident from the character for words itself: 言. Originally written 言, it represented a mouth ㅂ from which issued a mistake 辛 (an old form of 愆). Apparently, to correct this error, man changed 言 to 言. So today, with great care, his mouth 口 speaks its lines 亖, transforming soundwaves into words: 言.

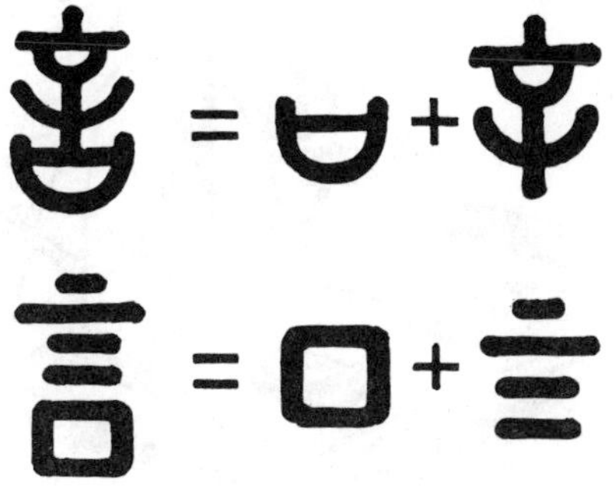

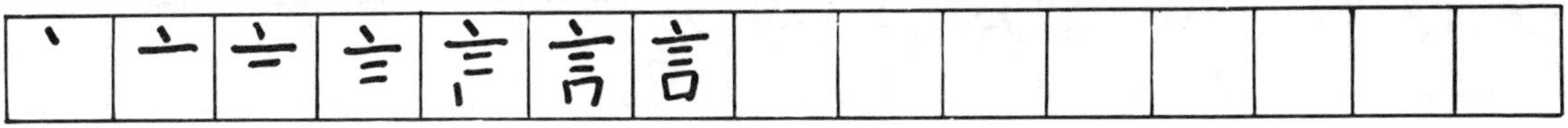

言辞	yán cí	one's words
言和	yán hé	make peace
言论	yán lùn	speech
言谈	yán tán	the way one speaks or the words one says
言行	yán xíng	words and deeds

言语	yán yǔ	spoken language
言不由衷	yán bù yóu zhōng	speak insincerely
言而无信	yán ér wú xìn	fail to keep faith
言过其实	yán guò qí shí	exaggerate
言听计从	yán tīng jì cóng	readily accept one's advice
言外之意	yán wài zhī yì	implications

Example:

他 言 行 不 一 致 。

Tā yán xíng bù yī zhì.

It means, "His words do not correspond with his actions."

信

xìn

believe;
trust;
letter

This character pictures a man 人 standing by his word 言, a fitting symbol for faith and trust: 信. Ancient forms show a man and mouth; also a heart and words, i.e., words from the heart - sincere and honest. As only man 人 can transmit his word by writing, 信 (man and word) also came to mean the written letter or epistle.

ノ 亻 亻 仁 仁 信 信 信 信

信封	xìn fēng	envelope
信奉	xìn fèng	believe in
信服	xìn fú	be convinced
信号	xìn hào	signal
信件	xìn jiàn	letter
信笺	xìn jiān	letter pad
信教	xìn jiào	believe in a religion
信赖	xìn lài	trust
信任	xìn rèn	have confidence in

信条	xìn tiáo	creed
信徒	xìn tú	disciple
信托	xìn tuō	trust
信箱	xìn xiāng	post box
信心	xìn xīn	confidence; faith
信仰	xìn yǎng	belief
信用	xìn yòng	trustworthiness
写信	xiě xìn	write letters

Example:

请 给 我 一 个 信 封 。

Qǐng gěi wǒ yī gè xìn fēng.

It means, "Please give me an envelope."

工 gōng

work;
labour;
skill

工 is a pictograph of the ancient workman's square or carpenter's ruler. By extension, it means work, labour or skill. An early form: 工 included three parallel lines traced with the square. Man has always had problems with work and remuneration. Instead of striving for prosperity through work, he works for prosperity through strife, as our picture of master and servant shows.

工厂	gōng chǎng	factory	工钱	gōng qián	service charges
工党	Gōng Dǎng	the Labour Party	工人	gōng rén	worker
工地	gōng dì	construction site	工业	gōng yè	industry
工夫	gōng fu	time; effort	工艺	gōng yì	technology
工具	gōng jù	tools	工资	gōng zī	wages
工会	gōng huì	trade union	工作	gōng zuò	job
工匠	gōng jiàng	craftsman	工程师	gōng chéng shī	engineer
工农	gōng nóng	workers and peasants	工业化	gōng yè huà	industralize
			工艺品	gōng yì pǐn	crafts

Example:

他 是 个 工 人 。
Tā shì gè gōng rén.

It means, "He is a worker."

左 **zuǒ**

left;
also a Chinese
surname

The character for left: 左 depicts the
hand ナ that holds the carpenter's
square エ — the left. The left hand ナ is
meant to help its more skilled correla-
tive member in manual work エ as, for
example, holding the ruler while the
right hand draws the line. 左 stands for
the direction left.

一 ナ 左 左 左

左边	zuǒ bian	left side
左面	zuǒ miàn	left side
左派	zuǒ pài	leftist
左倾	zuǒ qīng	left-leaning
左手	zuǒ shǒu	left hand
左翼	zuǒ yì	left wing

左右	zuǒ yòu	left and right
左右手	zuǒ yòu shǒu	the right-hand man
左右逢源	zuǒ yòu féng yuán	win advantages from both sides
左右为难	zuǒ yòu wéi nán	in a dilemma

Example:

他 用 左 手 写 字 。
Tā yòng zuǒ shǒu xiě zì.
It means, "He writes with his left hand."

54

右

yòu

right

The character for right: 右 is simply a hand 𠂇 and a mouth 口, signifying the hand you eat with — the right. 右 stands for the direction right.

一	𠂇	𠂇	右	右						

右边	yòu bian	right side		右手	yòu shǒu	right hand
右面	yòu miàn	right side		右翼	yòu yi	right wing
右派	yòu pài	rightist		向右	xiàng yòu	turn right
右倾	yòu qīng	right deviation				

Example:

他 向 右 转 。

Tā xiàng yòu zhuǎn.

It means, "He turns right."

舌

shé

tongue

"The tongue is like a sharp knife; it kills without drawing blood," so warns the Chinese proverb. Exemplifying this, early forms of the character show a forked tongue thrust viciously out of the mouth: 舌. It skilfully smoothens itself: 舌 and finally straightens: 舌 into the new form: 舌.

PENG

丿 一 干 千 舌 舌

舌尖	shé jiān	tip of the tongue
舌头	shé tou	tongue
舌音	shé yīn	lingual sounds
舌战	shé zhàn	heated discussion

Example:

辩 论 会 中 ， 双 方 展 开 舌 战 。
Biàn lùn huì zhōng, shuāng fāng zhǎn kāi shé zhàn.
It means, "Both sides are having a heated discussion at the debate."

56

话 （話）

huà

talk; speech; language

Man combined words 言 and tongue 舌 to produce 話, meaning speech or language. To emphasize the importance of weighing words before delivery and to caution against their indiscriminate proliferation, the Chinese proverb warns: "Water and words are easy to pour out but impossible to recover."

` 讠 讠 讠 讠 话 话 话

话别	huà bié	say goodbye
话柄	huà bǐng	subject for ridicule
话旧	huà jiù	talk about old times
话剧	huà jù	stage play

话题	huà tí	subject of a talk
话里有话	huà lǐ yǒu huà	there's more to it than what is merely said
笑话	xiào huà	joke

Example:

他 讲 话 很 大 声 。

Tā jiǎng huà hěn dà shēng.

It means, "He talks very loudly."

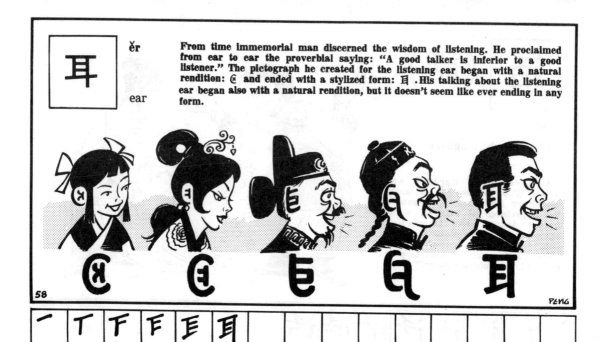

耳 ěr — ear

From time immemorial man discerned the wisdom of listening. He proclaimed from ear to ear the proverbial saying: "A good talker is inferior to a good listener." The pictograph he created for the listening ear began with a natural rendition: ᙦ and ended with a stylized form: 耳 . His talking about the listening ear began also with a natural rendition, but it doesn't seem like ever ending in any form.

58

PENG

一 丁 下 F F 耳

耳朵	ěr duo	ear	
耳光	ěr guāng	a box on the ear	
耳环	ěr huán	earrings	
耳机	ěr jī	earphones	
耳孔	ěr kǒng	earhole	
耳鸣	ěr míng	tinnitus	
耳目	ěr mù	informer	
耳塞	ěr sai	earplug	

耳屎	ěr shǐ	earwax
耳语	ěr yǔ	whisper
耳边风	ěr biān fēng	turn a deaf ear to
耳目一新	ěr mù yī xīn	pleasant change of atmosphere
耳闻目睹	ěr wén mù dǔ	what one hears and sees

Example:

他 的 耳 朵 很 灵 。
Tā de ěr duo hěn líng

It means, "He has sharp ears."

58

qǔ

take; select; seize

To secure a firm hold on a person the hand 又 is laid on the ear 耳. A hand on the ear, then, means to take hold of, to select or seize: 取. Pictured here are various characters extending a helping hand to demonstrate what 取 means.

一 丁 F F 耳 耳 取 取

取材	qǔ cái	acquire material (for writing)
取代	qǔ dài	replace
取道	qǔ dào	by way of; via
取得	qǔ dé	obtain
取缔	qǔ dì	ban; suppress
取决	qǔ jué	be decided by
取巧	qǔ qiǎo	resort to trickery

取舍	qǔ shě	make one's choice
取胜	qǔ shèng	score a success
取消	qǔ xiāo	cancel
取笑	qǔ xiào	make fun of
取长补短	qǔ cháng bǔ duǎn	learn from other's strong points to remedy one's weaknesses

Example:

他 取 消 一 个 宴 会 。

Tā qǔ xiāo yī gè yàn huì.

It means, "He has cancelled a dinner."

娶
qǔ
marry

取 means to select or obtain, i.e., figuratively taking hold of a person by the ear 耳 in the hand 又 . To select a woman 女 therefore means to marry: 娶 . Today, however, it is never wise for a man to select a wife in this way, for a hand on her ear definitely means a fist on his ear.

| 一 | 丁 | 下 | 下 | 耳 | 耳 | 耵 | 取 | 娶 | 娶 | 娶 | | | | |

| 娶亲 | qǔ qīn | marry (a woman); take a wife |

Example:

他 娶 了 亲 以 后 , 日 子 过 得 很 幸 福 。
Tā qǔ le qīn yǐ hòu, rì zǐ guò de hěn xìng fú.
It means, "He leads a happy life after marriage."

XIŌNG

兄

elder brother

The concept of "older brother" is suggested by the ideograph 兄 which combines person 人 with mouth 口. Ideally, 兄 represents a person 人 characterized by a large mouth 口, i.e., one who speaks with authority to exhort or correct a younger brother. Our picture shows what could happen in reality if big mouth of "older brother" went into action.

丶	冂	口	尸	兄											

| 兄弟 | xiōng dì | brothers |
| 兄长 | xiōng zhǎng | respectful form of address for an elder brother or a man friend |

| 兄弟之邦 | xiōng dì zhī bāng | fraternal states |
| 长兄 | zhǎng xiōng | elder brother |

Example:

我 有 很 多 兄 弟 姐 妹 。

Wǒ yǒu hěn duō xiōng dì jiě mèi.

It means, "I have many brothers and sisters."

61

BĀ

八

eight

In the etymological sense, 八 means to divide or separate. It is made up of two separate strokes, forming a symmetrical symbol 八. Probably because the number 8 can be easily divided and subdivided, 八 (to divide) came to stand for 8, the much-divisible number. The original seal form: ㄗㄩ, coincidentally, has 8 lines.

ノ	八													

八仙　　Bā Xiān　　The Eight Immortals
八月　　bā yuè　　August

八字　　bā zì　　Eight Characters (in four pairs, indicating the year, month, day and hour of a person's birth, each pair consisting of one Heavenly Stem and one Earthly Branch, used in fortune telling).

Example:

这 个 月 是 八 月 。
Zhè gè yuè shì bā yuè.
It means, "This month is August."

DUÌ

exchange;
barter

The character 兌 originally meant to speak, bless or rejoice. It was derived from older brother's 兄 dissipation of effluent breath 八 into words of encouragement: 兌 involving the exchange of words. With money talking louder than words in man's affluent society, there arose the need to exchange the old meaning for a new one. Today, 兌 means to exchange money or to barter.

兌付	duì fù	cash (a cheque, etc)
兌换	duì huàn	exchange
兌现	duì xiàn	pay cash
兌换表	duì huàn biǎo	exchange table

Example:

他 去 银 行 兌 现 支 票 。

Tā qù yíng háng duì xiàn zhī piào.

It means, "He went to the bank to cash a cheque."

63

说（說）

SHUŌ speak; theory; story

說 is a character that speaks for itself; it means to speak, i.e., to exchange 兌 words 言. It is an ideograph of elder brother 兄 separating his words 八, exchanging them in speech 说. It can also mean theory, opinion or story as, for example: 小说 or "small story", a novel.

丶 讠 讠 讠 讠 说 说 说 说

说穿	shuō chuān	expose
说法	shuō fǎ	way of saying a thing
说服	shuō fú	persuade; convince
说话	shuō huà	talk
说谎	shuō huǎng	tell a lie
说教	shuō jiào	preach
说理	shuō lǐ	reason things out
说媒	shuō méi	act as matchmaker
说明	shuō míng	explain

说亲	shuō qīn	act as matchmaker
说情	shuō qíng	plead for mercy for somebody
说笑	shuō xiào	chatting and laughing
说不定	shuō bu dìng	perhaps
说大话	shuō dà huà	talk big; boast
说得来	shuō de lái	can get along
说到做到	shuō dào zuò dào	do what one says
小说	xiǎo shuō	novel

Example:

他 不 能 说 服 我 。
Tā bù néng shuō fú wǒ.

It means, "He cannot convince me."

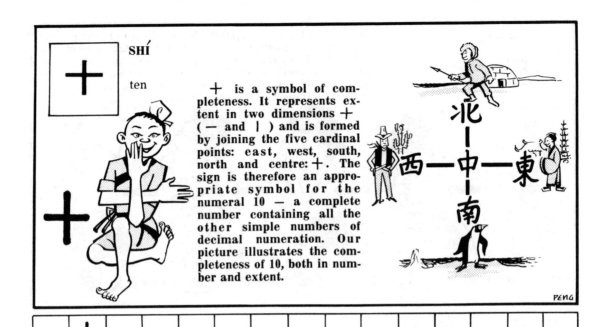

SHÍ

十 ten

十 is a symbol of completeness. It represents extent in two dimensions 十 (一 and ｜) and is formed by joining the five cardinal points: east, west, south, north and centre: 十. The sign is therefore an appropriate symbol for the numeral 10 — a complete number containing all the other simple numbers of decimal numeration. Our picture illustrates the completeness of 10, both in number and extent.

一	十											

十分	shí fēn	very; fully	十字架	shí zì jià	cross
十万	shí wàn	one hundred thousand	十拿九稳	shí ná jiǔ wěn	90 per cent certain of
十月	shí yuè	October	十全十美	shí quán shí měi	faultless
十足	shí zú	100 per cent	十之八九	shí zhī bā jiǔ	ineight or nine cases out of ten
十二月	shí èr yuè	December			
十一月	shí yī yuè	November	十字路口	shí zì lù kǒu	crossroad

Example:

他 对 你 的 工作 十 分 满 意 。
Tā duì nǐ de gōng zuò shí fēn mǎn yì.
It means, "He is very satisfied with your work."

65

GǓ

古

old; ancient;
also a Chinese
surname

This character 古 is applicable to that which has passed through ten 十 mouths 口 — a tradition dating back ten generations. It includes anything very old, ancient, of antiquity — whether valuable, invaluable or valueless. Our picture illustrates the process of passing through ten mouths something of questionable value.

PENG

一 十 十 古 古

古巴	Gǔ Bā	Cuba	古老	gǔ lǎo	ancient
古代	gǔ dài	ancient times	古人	gǔ rén	our forefathers
古典	gǔ diǎn	classical	古书	gǔ shū	ancient book
古董	gǔ dǒng	antique	古玩	gǔ wán	curio
古怪	gǔ guài	peculiar; strange	古装	gǔ zhuāng	ancient costume
古国	gǔ guó	ancient state	古色古香	gǔ sè gǔ xiāng	quaint
古迹	gǔ jì	historic monuments	古为今用	gǔ wéi jīn yòng	make the past serve the present
古旧	gǔ jiù	archaic			

Example:

罗 马 有 许 多 古 迹 。

Luó Mǎ yǒu xǔ duō gǔ jì.

It means, "There are many historical monuments in Rome."

JÌ

计 (計)

calculate;
plan;
scheme

Sayings 言 in tens 十 implies the ability to calculate 計 – to know how to enumerate 言 the ten numbers 十 of the decimal system. By extension, 計 means to reckon, to plan, to scheme. Below we show a pair of scheming, calculating characters, counting their chickens.

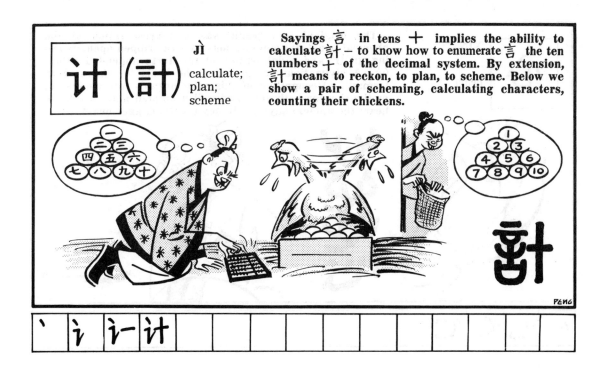

丶	讠	讠一	计												

计策	jì cè	stratagem	
计划	jì huà	plan	
计较	jì jiào	haggle over	
计谋	jì móu	scheme	
计时	jì shí	reckon by time	
计算	jì suàn	calculate	

计议	jì yì	deliberate; talk over
计算机	jì suàn jī	calculator
生计	shēng jì	livelihood
家庭计划	jiā tíng jì huà	family planning

Example:

这 个 计 算 机 多 少 钱 ?
Zhè gè jì suàn jī duō shǎo qián?

It means, "How much does this calculator cost?"

67

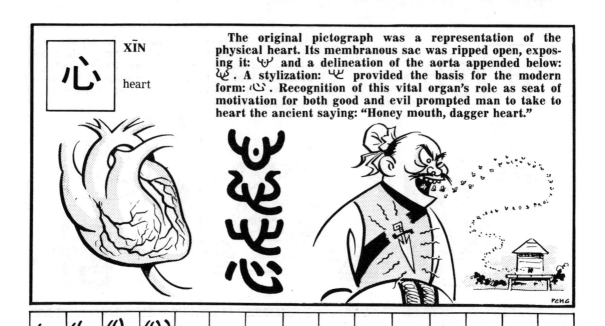

XĪN

心

heart

The original pictograph was a representation of the physical heart. Its membranous sac was ripped open, exposing it: and a delineation of the aorta appended below: . A stylization: provided the basis for the modern form: 心 . Recognition of this vital organ's role as seat of motivation for both good and evil prompted man to take to heart the ancient saying: "Honey mouth, dagger heart."

心爱	xīn ài	dear
心得	xīn dé	personal insight
心烦	xīn fán	vexed
心腹	xīn fù	trusted subordinate
心理	xīn lǐ	psychology
心事	xīn shì	things that weigh on one's mind
心目	xīn mù	frame of mind
心情	xīn qíng	state of mind

心思	xīn si	thought; idea
心甘情愿	xīn gān qíng yùan	willingly
心花怒放	xīn huā nù fàng	elated
心神不定	xīn shén bù dìng	restless mind
心心相印	xīn xīn xiāng yìn	have mutual affinity
灰心	huī xīn	disheartened

Example:

不 要 因 失 败 而 灰 心 。
Bù yào yīn shī bài ér huī xīn
It means, "Do not be disheartened by failures."

68

怒

NÙ

anger; rage; passion

The very sinister structure of 怒, meaning anger or passion, constitutes a warning to man, for 怒 was secured by bonding slave 奴 to heart 心. It cautions against giving way to anger or passion and becoming slave and handmaid 奴 to the dictates of the heart 心.

ㄥ	ㄠ	女	奻	奴	奴	怒	怒	怒					

怒斥	nù chì	rebuke angrily
怒吼	nù hǒu	howl
怒火	nù huǒ	fury
怒气	nù qì	rage; fury
怒容	nù róng	angry look
怒色	nù sè	angry look

怒视	nù shì	stare at someone or something in anger
怒冲冲	nù chōng chōng	angrily
怒发冲冠	nù fà chōng guan	in utmost anger
怒目而视	nù mù ér shì	stare angrily
愤怒	fèn nù	angry

Example:

他 们 两 人 怒 目 而 视 。

Tā men liǎng rén nù mù ér shì.

It means, "They stare angrily at each other."

69

PÀ

fear

The character for fear has, for radical, 忄 — a variant of heart 心. The phonetic, sound component 白 (white) collaborates with the radical, 心 (heart) to instil the idea of fear into this character: 怕, which literally means: "white heart", i.e., fear or lack of courage. Sometimes a "white heart" can inspire the bold deeds of a "lion-heart" as our picture shows.

'	忄	忄	忄	忄	怕	怕	怕					

怕人	pà rén	terrifying	怕死	pà sǐ	fear death
怕生	pà shēng	(of a child) shy with strangers	怕羞	pà xiū	bashful; shy
怕事	pà shì	afraid of getting into trouble	害怕	hài pà	scared

Example:

她 很 怕 我 。

Tā hěn pà wǒ.

It means, "She is scared of me."

70

SHĒN

body

This character originally meant "pregnant"; it pictured a human figure with prominent belly and one leg thrust forward to support and balance the body: 久 . The modern form: 身 also means "the human body" - either male or female, ordinary or outstanding. We show a couple of outstanding ones - outstanding in "body", not in form or figure.

丿 亻 冂 白 白 身 身

身边	shēn biān	at (or by) one's side
身材	shēn cái	figure (body)
身分	shēn fèn	social status
身价	shēn jià	social status
身躯	shēn qū	body; stature
身世	shēn shì	one's lot

身体	shēn tǐ	body
身心	shēn xīn	body and mind
身孕	shēn yùn	pregnancy
身分证	shēn fēn zhèng	identity card
身临其境	shēn lín qí jìng	be present on the spot

Example:

他 的 身 体 很 弱 。
Tā de shēn tǐ hěn ruò.

It means, "He is very weak."

zì

self;
oneself

Because the nose sticks out most from the face — sometimes too far out — it characterizes the person and symbolizes his personality. A pictographic representation of the nose therefore personifies, not the nose, but "self" or "oneself". Our picture emphasizes the dominant role of the nose in a confrontation of personalities.

ノ　亻　宀　白　自　自

自白	zì bái	self-confession	
自卑	zì bēi	inferiority complex; self-abased	
自动	zì dòng	automatic	
自杀	zì shā	commit suicide	
自首	zì shǒu	give oneself up	
自传	zì zhuàn	autobiography	
自己	zì jǐ	oneself	
自立	zì lì	independent	
自满	zì mǎn	complacent	

自由	zì yóu	freedom
自愿	zì yuàn	voluntarily
自来水	zì lái shuǐ	tap water
自暴自弃	zì bào zì qì	self-forsaking
自告奋勇	zì gào fèn yǒng	volunteer one's service
自高自大	zì gāo zì dà	conceited; egoistic
自食其力	zì shí qí lì	self-supporting
自相矛盾	zì xiāng máo dùn	self-contradiction

Example:

他 很 自 私 。

Tā hěn zì sī.

It means, "He is very selfish."

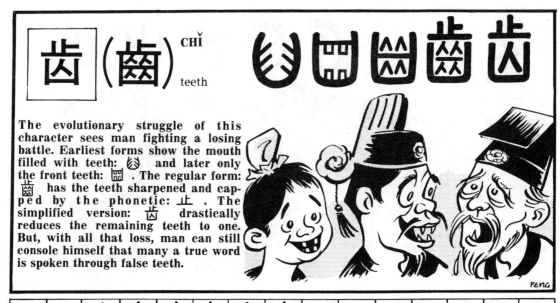

齿 (齒) CHǏ teeth

The evolutionary struggle of this character sees man fighting a losing battle. Earliest forms show the mouth filled with teeth: 齒 and later only the front teeth: 齒 . The regular form: 齒 has the teeth sharpened and capped by the phonetic: 止 . The simplified version: 齿 drastically reduces the remaining teeth to one. But, with all that loss, man can still console himself that many a true word is spoken through false teeth.

齿轮	chǐ lún	gear-wheel	齿龈	chǐ yín	the gums
齿腔	chǐ qiāng	dental cavity	牙齿	yá chǐ	tooth
齿痛	chǐ tòng	toothache			

Example:

他 的 牙 齿 痛 。
Tā de yá chǐ tòng.

It means, "He has a toothache."

止 **ZHǏ**

halt; stop

Although this character is a crude representation of the motionless foot, with the five toes reduced to three, it does not stand for "foot". Its meanings are derived by extension and include: to halt, stop or stand still. Our illustration shows how, in an emergency, the foot can come in handy to express the idea of "Stop!"

一 ト ⺊ 止

止步	zhǐ bù	halt; stop
止境	zhǐ jìng	limit; end
止渴	zhǐ kě	quench thirst
止咳	zhǐ ké	relieve a cough
止痛	zhǐ tòng	allay pains
止血	zhǐ xuè	stop bleeding

止咳药	zhǐ ké yào	cough mixture
停止	tíng zhǐ	halt; stop
终止	zhōng zhǐ	put an end to; cease
望梅止渴	wàng méi zhǐ kě	gaze at plums to quench one's thirst; vain hopes

Example:

酸 梅 可 以 止 渴 。
Suān méi kě yǐ zhǐ kě
It means, "Sour plums can quench your thirst."

ZÚ

foot

The character:  apparently pictures the knee-cap: ○ resting on the foot: 止. The full circle: ○ suggests completion and rest, as opposed to motion. The modern form: 足, signifying foot at rest, is applicable to feet in general. And feet are generally at rest, as our example shows.

丨	冂	口	무	무	足	足						

足够	zú gòu	enough
足迹	zú jì	footprint
足金	zú jīn	pure gold
足球	zú qiú	soccer; football
足下	zú xià	polite form of address between friends

足球队	zú qiú duì	soccer team
足球迷	zú qiú mí	soccer fan
满足	mǎn zú	satisfied; satisfy
手足情深	shǒu zú qíng shēn	brotherly affection

Example:

他 喜 欢 看 足 球 赛 。

Tā xǐ huān kàn zú qiú sài.

It means, "He likes to watch football matches."

75

疋 PǏ

piece of cloth;
bale or roll

This character:  has an uncompleted circle: ꝿ flowing into a foot: 止, signifying the foot in motion. In this sense, it is now obsolete - probably because feet today are seldom in motion. The character is now mainly applied to a bale, bolt or roll of cloth, which is undone by a regular motion of turning it over and over again. Our picture illustrates both obsolete and modern meanings of 疋.

一 丁 乛 乛 疋

| 疋头 | pǐ tóu | piece goods |
| 一疋布 | yī pǐ bù | one piece of cloth |

Example:

她 买 了 一 疋 布 。

Tā mǎi le yī pǐ bù.

It means, "She bought a piece of cloth."

76

BÙ

步

step;
pace

This character for "step" or "pace" is an ideograph of a right foot and a left foot, one following the other in close succession, graphically conveying the idea of walking or taking steps. Such steps, however, could be in the wrong direction; our picture presents a good example of this.

| 一 | 卜 | 止 | 止 | 牛 | 步 | 步 | | | | | | |

步兵	bù bīng	infantry	步行	bù xíng	go on foot
步步	bù bù	step by step	步骤	bù zhòu	move; measure
步调	bù diào	pace or speed (in walking or running)	步步高升	bù bù gāo shēng	rise step by step (promotions)
步伐	bù fá	pace	进步	jìng bù	progress; improve
步法	bù fǎ	footwork	跑步	pǎo bù	jog
步枪	bù qiāng	rifle	散步	sàn bù	take a stroll

Example:

他 的 功 课 进 步 得 很 快 。
Tā de gōng kè jìn bù de hěn kuài.
It means, "His lessons have improved rapidly."

77

正 **ZHÈNG**

straight;
upright;
correct;
exact

The character: 正 shows a foot: 止 (meaning "stop") with a straight line above it. It signifies arrival and stopping (止) at the line or proper limit (一) without going astray. It is also an ideograph of a foot walking in a straight line: 正 . Hence the extended meanings: straight, upright, proper, correct, exact.

一 丁 下 正 正

正常	zhèng cháng	normal
正当	zhèng dàng	proper; rightful
正派	zhèng pài	upright; decent
正确	zhèng què	correct; right
正式	zhèng shì	official
正统	zhèng tǒng	orthodox
正义	zhèng yì	justice

正月	zhēng yuè	January
正常化	zhèng cháng huà	normalize
正规军	zhèng guī jūn	regular army
改正	gǎi zhèng	correct
纠正	jiū zhèng	amend; correct
改邪归正	gǎi xié guī zhèng	turn over a new leaf

Example:

那 犯 人 已 改 邪 归 正 。
Nà fàn rén yǐ gǎi xié guī zhèng.

It means, "That convict has turned over a new leaf."

是 SHÌ

是 right; yes; am, are, is

This ideograph locates the sun: 日 over the character for right or correct: 正 (modified to 疋). It depicts the sun: 日 exactly on the meridian: 是. The sun is here taken as the standard for correctness. Hence the idea of "right; yes; am, are, is."

| 丨 | 冂 | 冃 | 日 | 旦 | 昰 | 昰 | 昆 | 是 | | | | | |

是的	shì de	yes; right
是非	shì fēi	right and wrong
是否	shì fǒu	whether or not?
是故	shì gù	for this reason
不是	bù shì	not so

Example:

这 把 雨 伞 不 是 我 的 。
Zhè bǎ yǔ sǎn bù shì wǒ de.
It means, "This umbrella is not mine."

79

ZŎU

walk;
run;
hasten;
depart

In the original seal form: 㐬 the upper part: 夭 (or 土) represents a man: 大 bending his head: 丿 forward to walk rapidly. The lower part: 止 (or 龰) means "to stop." This combination of bending and stopping indicates walking. The movement is also suggested by the bending: 夭 (土) of the toes or foot: 止 (龰) in swift walking. Pictured here are a host of characters - walking, running, fleeing - all bending forward but not stopping.

一 十 土 キ 卡 走 走

走动	zǒu dòng	move around
走访	zǒu fǎng	have an interview with
走狗	zǒu gǒu	running dog; lackey
走廊	zǒu láng	corridor
走漏	zǒu lòu	leak out (secret)
走路	zǒu lù	walk
走私	zǒu sī	smuggling

走失	zǒu shī	be lost
走兽	zǒu shòu	beast
走向	zǒu xiàng	walk towards
走样	zǒu yàng	change in shape
走卒	zǒu zú	lackey
走漏风声	zǒu lòu fēng shēng	leak out a secret
走马看花	zǒu mǎ kàn huā	taking a hurried glance

Example:

他 走 路 去 学 校 。
Tā zǒu lù qù xué xiào.

It means, "He walks to school."

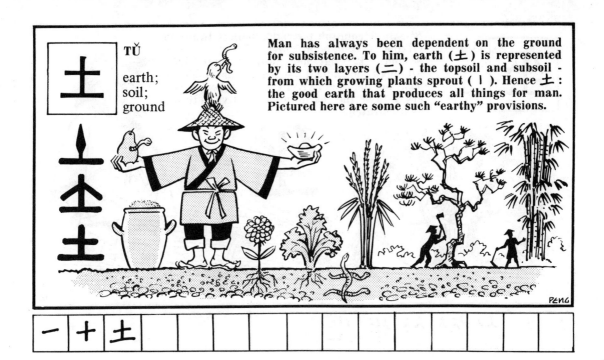

TŬ

earth;
soil;
ground

Man has always been dependent on the ground for subsistence. To him, earth (土) is represented by its two layers (二) - the topsoil and subsoil - from which growing plants sprout (丨). Hence 土: the good earth that produces all things for man. Pictured here are some such "earthy" provisions.

一　十　土

土产	tǔ chǎn	local commodities (natural produces)
土地	tǔ dì	land
土匪	tǔ fěi	bandit
土话	tǔ huà	local dialect
土壤	tǔ rǎng	soil

土人	tǔ rén	native
土质	tǔ zhì	property of soil
土包子	tǔ bāo zi	country bumpkin
土耳其	Tǔ Ěr Qí	Turkey
土木工程	Tǔ mù gōng chéng	civil engineering
泥土	ní tǔ	soil, earth

Example:

这 是 一 块 肥 沃 的 土 地 。
Zhè shì yí kuài féi wò de tǔ dì.
It means, "This piece of land is fertile."

ZUÒ

坐

to sit;
a seat

坐, the ideograph for "sit", depicts two men talking face-to-face (人人), sitting on the ground (土) but not quite down-to-earth. Although the radical 土 (earth) provides the base for the men (人人) to "sit" (坐) on, it can prove to be the root of unproductive activity, as illustrated.

PENG

丿	人	亻	从	坐	坐	坐							

坐牢	zuò láo	be imprisoned	坐井观天	zuò jǐng guān tiān	(literally) see the sky from the bottom of a well—take a narrow view of
坐落	zuò luò	locate; situate			
坐视	zuò shì	sit by and watch			
坐位	zuò wei	seat			
坐下	zuò xià	sit down	请坐	qǐng zuò	please sit down
坐立不安	zuò lì bù ān	be fidgety			

Example:

他 请 客 人 坐 下 。

Tā qǐng kè rén zuò xià

It means, "He invited the guest to sit down."

82

CHŪ

go out;
issue;
produce

Originally, 出 represented a stalk (屮) thrusting itself out of its receptacle (凵) - the ground - and bursting out in full bloom. This verbal character places emphasis on the action "out". Translating this action visually, our picture shows "out" being expressed, not only in the active voice, but also in the passive voice.

| 凵 | 凵 | 屮 | 出 | 出 | | | | | | | | | |

出版	chū bǎn	publish	出门	chū mén	be away from home
出产	chū chǎn	produce	出去	chū qù	go out
出丑	chū chǒu	make a fool of oneself	出身	chū shēn	family background
出国	chū guó	go abroad	出现	chū xiàn	appear; emerge
出境	chū jìng	leave a country	出乎意料	chū hū yì lìao	unexpected
出口	chū kǒu	export	出人头地	chū rén tóu dì	stand above others
出来	chū lai	come out	出生入死	chū shēng rù sǐ	go through thick and thin
出卖	chū mài	betray			

Example:

他 出 版 了 一 本 书 。
Tā chū bǎn le yì běn shū.

It means, "He has published a book."

生 SHĒNG

produce;
bear;
grow

The earth (土), producing a plant (屮), lays the groundwork for growth (坐). Hence the modified form: 生, meaning to produce, bear or grow. Man, born imperfect, grows in different ways and directions. Pictured here are examples from three generations.

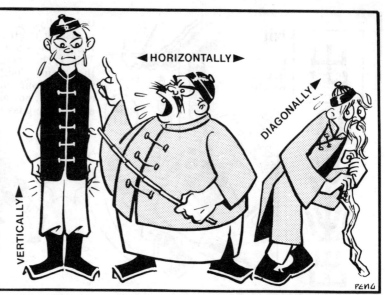

◄ HORIZONTALLY ►

VERTICALLY ►

DIAGONALLY

PENG

丿 ㇒ 仁 牛 生

生病	shēng bìng	fall ill	
生存	shēng cún	survive	
生动	shēng dòng	vivid	
生活	shēng huó	livelihood	
生理	shēng lǐ	physiology	
生命	shēng mìng	life	
生气	shēng qì	angry	
生日	shēng ri	birthday	

生疏	shēng shū	unfamiliar
生物	shēng wù	biology
生效	shēng xiào	become effective
生意	shēng yì	business
生硬	shēng yìng	rigid
生长	shēng zhǎng	grow up
生气勃勃	shēng qì bó bó	full of vigour and vitality

Example:

明 天 是 她 的 生 日 。

Míng tiān shì tā de shēng ri.

It means, "Tomorrow is her birthday."

姓

XÌNG

surname

The character 姓, comprising 女 (woman) and 生 (born), literally means: "born of woman". It suggests that in some remote, forgotten era man, born of woman, got his name from the mother. Hence 姓: "surname". We introduce here Mama Li's (李) family from the remote past, but we've forgotten Papa's insignificant surname.

| | | | | | | | | | | | | |
|く|ㄑ|女|女|妒|妒|姓|姓| | | | | |

姓名	xìng míng	surname and name	百姓	bǎi xìng	common people
姓谱	xìng pǔ	genealogical record; family register	贵姓	guì xìng	what is your surname?
姓氏	xìng shì	surname			

Example:

请 问 您 姓 什 么 ?

Qǐng wèn nín xìng shěn me ?

It means, "What is your surname, please?"

贝 (貝) BÈI
shells; valuables

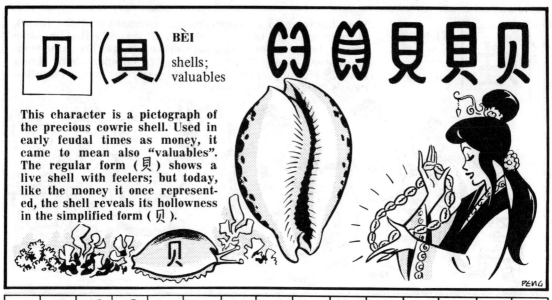

This character is a pictograph of the precious cowrie shell. Used in early feudal times as money, it came to mean also "valuables". The regular form (貝) shows a live shell with feelers; but today, like the money it once represented, the shell reveals its hollowness in the simplified form (贝).

丨	冂	贝	贝										

贝雕	bèi diāo	shell carving	贝子	bèi zi	cowries—used as currency in ancient times
贝壳	bèi ké	shell			
贝类	bèi lèi	shellfish	宝贝	bǎo bèi	precious; darling
贝玉	bèi yù	valuables; gems			

Example:

这 贝 壳 很 美 。
Zhè bèi ké hěn měi.
It means, "This shell is very beautiful."

86

贱 (賤)

JIÀN cheap; mean; worthless

Two spears: 戔 shattering and destroying the value of shells: 貝 , once used as money, conveys the idea of cheap, worthless, mean or humble. Man applied this word to anything of little value, uttering the proverbial saying: "Cheap things are of little value; valuable things are not cheap". In mock humility, he applied it also to himself.

PENG

丨	冂	贝	贝	贝	贝	贱	贱	贱					

贱价	jiàn jia	cheap; low-priced
贱卖	jiàn mài	cheap-sale
贱物（货）	jiàn wù (huò)	cheap and common things; inferior quality goods

贫贱	pín jiàn	poor and humble
贱骨头	jiàn gú tóu	miserable (or contemptible) wretch

Example:

她 出 生 贫 贱 。
Tā chū shēng pín jiàn.

It means, "She comes from a poor and humble family."

贵(貴)

GUÌ

expensive;
dear;
honourable

A basket or container: 史 (or 虫) filled with precious cowries: 貝 (once used as money) means dear or expensive. By extension, it also means high-class or honourable. In this connection, humble self (贱) thanks honourable readers (贵) for their appreciation and interest in the Bilingual Page.

丶	冖	口	中	虫	虫	弗	贵	贵				

贵宾	guì bīn	guest of honour	贵人	guì rén	distinguished person
贵妇	guì fù	noblewoman			
贵国	guì guó	your nation (a polite expression)	贵姓	guì xìng	your name, please
			贵重	guì zhòng	valuable; precious
贵贱	guì jiàn	the eminent and the humble	贵族	guì zú	aristocrat; noble
			宝贵	bǎo guì	precious

Example:

英 国 有 许 多 贵 族 人 家 。

Yīng Guó yǒu xǔ duō guì zú rén jiā.

It means, "There are many aristocratic families in England."

买 (買) MǍI buy

This ideograph is made up of a net: 罒 (modified from 网) and shells: 貝 (money-cowrie). 買 means to buy, i.e., net of (罒) goods, paying the price in cowries (貝). This is often done with bargain offers. The simplified form: 买 offered in place of the regular form: 買 may not seem quite a bargain, but we'll buy it.

一 ㄱ ㄋ 彐 乑 买

买方	mǎi fāng	buyer	
买好	mǎi hǎo	try to win some-body's favour	
买价	mǎi jià	buying price	
买卖	mǎi mài	buying and selling	

买通	mǎi tōng	bribe; buy over
买主	mǎi zhǔ	buyer
买空卖空	mǎi kōng mài kōng	speculate (in stocks, etc.)

Example:

他 是 这 辆 新 车 的 买 主 。

Tā shì zhè liàng xīn chē de mǎi zhǔ.

It means, "He is the buyer of this new car."

卖（賣）　MÀI　sell

賣 is derived by loading 買 (the business of netting in cowries) with 士 (out, a contraction of 出). Hence 賣 means to sell, i.e., to put out or push (士 or 出) goods and netting in (罒 or 网) cowrie-money (貝). Our picture exposes the fishy business of pushing and netting.

一　十　士　吉　击　圭　卖　卖

卖唱	mài chàng	sing for a living
卖方	mài fāng	seller
卖国	mài guó	betray one's country
卖价	mài jià	selling price
卖力	mài lì	spare no effort
卖命	mài mìng	sweat one's guts out
卖弄	mài nòng	show off
卖笑	mài xiào	prostitution

卖艺	mài yì	make a living as a performer
卖淫	mài yín	prostitution
卖国贼	mài guó zéi	traitor
卖人情	mài rén qíng	grant a favour
卖身契	mài shēn qì	indenture by which one sells oneself or family
出卖	chū mài	betray
非卖品	fēi mài pǐn	not for sale
拍卖	pāi mài	sale by auction

Example:

他 出 卖 了 自 己 的 哥 哥 。
Tā chū mài le zì jǐ de gē gē
It means, "He has betrayed his own brother."

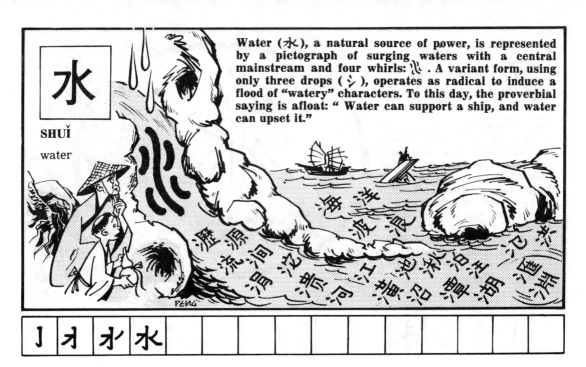

水

SHUǏ

water

Water (水), a natural source of power, is represented by a pictograph of surging waters with a central mainstream and four whirls: 水. A variant form, using only three drops (氵), operates as radical to induce a flood of "watery" characters. To this day, the proverbial saying is afloat: " Water can support a ship, and water can upset it."

亅	才	水	水									

水彩	shuǐ cǎi	water colour
水池	shuǐ chí	pond; pool
水沟	shuǐ gōu	drain; ditch
水管	shuǐ guǎn	water pipe
水果	shuǐ guǒ	fruit
水库	shuǐ kù	reservoir; dam
水泥	shuǐ ní	cement
水手	shuǐ shǒu	sailor; seaman
水塔	shuǐ tǎ	water tower

水星	Shuǐ Xīng	Mercury
水银	shuǐ yín	mercury
水灾	shuǐ zāi	flood
水龙头	shuǐ lóng tóu	tap; faucet
水深火热	shuǐ shēn huǒ rè	(figuratively) an abyss of suffering
水蒸气	shuǐ zhēng qì	steam
水泄不通	shuǐ xiè bù tōng	(figuratively) very crowded
喝水	hē shuǐ	drink water

Example:

吃 水 果 对 身 体 有 益 。

Chī shuǐ guǒ duì shēn tǐ yǒu yì.

It means, "Eating fruits is good for our health."

永 YǑNG

everlasting;
perpetual;
forever

One generation comes and another goes, but water flows on incessantly in a continuous cycle. From this unceasing flow of water came the ideograph for "everlasting": 永 - a variation of water (水), with foams and ripples added: 沭. 永 will long be remembered as the "everlasting" character that embodies the eight fundamental strokes used in calligraphy.

丶	亅	汀	永	永

永生	yǒng shēng	eternal life	永别	yǒng bié	part forever
永远	yǒng yuǎn	forever; everlasting	永不	yǒng bù	never
永不分离	yǒng bù fēn lí	inseparable	永固	yǒng gù	permanently fixed
永垂不朽	yǒng chuí bù xiǔ	eternal glory	永恒	yǒng héng	eternal; everlasting
			永久	yǒng jiǔ	permanent

Example:

他 们 的 爱 情 是 永 恒 的 。
Tā men de ài qíng shì yǒng héng de.
It means, "Their love is everlasting."

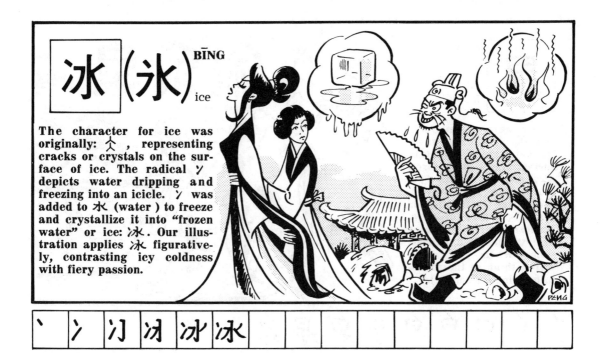

冰 (冰) BĪNG
ice

The character for ice was originally: 㐅 , representing cracks or crystals on the surface of ice. The radical 冫 depicts water dripping and freezing into an icicle. 冫 was added to 水 (water) to freeze and crystallize it into "frozen water" or ice: 冰 . Our illustration applies 冰 figuratively, contrasting icy coldness with fiery passion.

丶　冫　冫　冫　冰　冰

冰雹	bīng báo	hailstones
冰川	bīng chuān	glacier
冰岛	Bīng dǎo	Iceland
冰冻	bīng dòng	freeze
冰块	bīng kuài	ice-cube
冰冷	bīng lěng	ice-cold
冰凉	bīng liáng	ice-cold

冰山	bīng shān	iceberg
冰水	bīng shuǐ	ice-water
冰箱	bīng xiāng	refrigerator
冰淇淋	bīng qí lín	ice-cream
冰上运动	bīng shàng yùn dòng	ice-sports
冰天雪地	bīng tiān xuě dì	a world of ice and snow

Example:

她 喜 欢 吃 冰 淇 淋 。
Tā xǐ huān chī bīng qí lín.
It means, "She likes ice-cream."

QUÁN

泉

spring;
fountain

The early forms: and show water gushing out from a mountain spring. The modern form: 泉, distilled from 白 (pure) and 水 (water), symbolizes the fountain or spring - source of pure, wholesome drinking water and the inspired expression: "When you drink water, think of the mountain spring (or source)."

泉水	quán shuǐ	spring water
泉源	quán yuán	source of spring; source
喷泉	pēn quán	fountain

Example:

这 个 喷 泉 很 美 。
Zhè gè pēn quán hěn měi .

It means, "This is a very beautiful fountain."

94

雨

YǓ

rain

雨 , the character for rain, is a picture of raindrops (= =) falling vertically down (|) from a cloud (冂) in the heavens (一). Not all welcome the rain as showers of blessing from heaven for, as the saying goes, "The farmer hopes for rain, the traveller for fine weather."

雨点	yǔ diǎn	raindrop
雨季	yǔ jì	rainy season
雨量	yǔ liàng	rainfall
雨伞	yǔ sǎn	umbrella
雨水	yǔ shuǐ	rain water
雨天	yǔ tiān	rainy day
雨衣	yǔ yi	raincoat

雨过天晴	yǔ guò tiān qíng	the sun shines again after the rain
雨后春笋	yǔ hòu chūn sǔn	(spring up like) bamboo shoots after a spring rain
下雨	xià yǔ	raining

Example:

下 雨 了 ， 快 进 来 吧 ！

Xià yǔ le, kuài jìn lái ba!

It means, "It's raining, come in quickly!"

漏 LÒU

leak

The original character 屚 places rain 雨 under roof 尸 (abbreviation of 屋, house), enforcing the idea of "leak" - rain seeping through the roof into the house. The modern form reinforces the concept by adding more water in the form of the radical: 氵 (water): 漏.

`、 冫 氵 氵 沪 沪 沪 沪 渭 漏 漏 漏 漏 漏`

漏电	lòu diàn	leakage of e'ectri-city
漏洞	lòu dòng	flaw; loophole
漏斗	lòu dǒu	funnel for liquids
漏风	lòu fēng	air leak
漏光	lòu guāng	light leak

漏税	lòu shuì	evade taxation
漏雨	lòu yǔ	rain leaking through
漏风声	lòu fēng shēng	leak out a secret
漏洞百出	lòu dòng bǎi chū	full of loopholes
失漏	shī lòu	lose track of

Example:

他 漏 了 一 条 重 要 新 闻 。
Tā lòu le yì tiáo zhòng yào xīn wén.
It means, "He missed an important piece of news."

96

云 (雲) YÚN
cloud

When the humid and warm vapours (乙 or 厶) rise (上 or 二) and reach the colder regions, they condense and form clouds: 云 . Loading the clouds (云) with rain (雨) produces the regular form: 雲 . The simplified version relieves the clouds (雲) of their load, reverting the character to its original form: 云 .

一 二 云 云

云彩	yún cǎi	cloud
云层	yún céng	layers of cloud
云集	yún jí	gather together in crowds
云外	yún wài	beyond the clouds
云雾	yún wù	mist; fog
云霞	yún xiá	rosy clouds
云霄	yún xiāo	the skies
云烟	yún yān	cloud and mist

云消雾散	yún xiāo wù sàn	the clouds have cleared and the mist dispersed— (figuratively) troubles have been cleared up
白云	bái yún	white clouds
浮云	fú yún	passing cloud
乌云满布	wū yún mǎn bù	black clouds gather in the sky

Example:

天 上 有 朵 朵 白 云 。

Tiān shàng yǒu duǒ duǒ bái yún.

It means, "Billows of white clouds float in the sky."

97

雪 XUĚ

snow

The seal character 霅 associates rain 雨 with broom 彗. The modern character 雪 relates rain 雨 to hand ⺕ (a contraction of 彗, broom). Both versions fittingly symbolize snow, i.e., rain 雨 which can be taken up in the hand (⺕) or swept away by a broom (彗).

一 ⼁ 厂 帀 雨 雨 雪 雨 雪 雪 雪

雪白	xuě bái	snow-white	雪球	xuě qiú	snowball
雪崩	xuě bēng	snowslide	雪人	xuě rén	snowman
雪恨	xuě hèn	avenge	雪山	xuě shān	snow-covered mountain
雪花	xuě huā	snowflake			
雪茄	xuě jiā	cigar	雪花膏	xuě huā gāo	vanishing cream
雪景	xuě jǐng	snow scenery	雪中送炭	xuě zhōng sòng tàn	(figuratively) timely assistance
雪亮	xuě liàng	bright as snow	下雪	xià xuě	to snow

Example:

冬 天 ， 小 孩 子 喜 欢 造 雪 人 。

Dōng tiān,　xiǎo hái zi xǐ huān zào xuě rén.

It means, "In winter, children like to make snowmen."

98

电（電）

DIÀN lightning; electricity

A streak of lightning （电） amidst the falling rain （雨） forged the character for lightning: 電 . Lightning being a visible discharge of electricity, 電 came to mean also electricity. 電 takes the path of least resistance, discharging eight of its thirteen strokes to transform itself into the simplified form: 电 .

雹 雷 電 电

丨 冂 冃 日 电

电报	diàn bào	telegram; cable
电池	diàn chí	battery
电工	diàn gōng	electrician
电话	diàn huà	telephone
电流	diàn liú	electric current
电脑	diàn nǎo	computer
电视	diàn shì	television
电梯	diàn tī	elevator
电线	diàn xiàn	wire; cable

电讯	diàn xùn	telegraphic message
电影	diàn yǐng	movie-show; film
电唱机	diàn chàng jī	record player
电单车	diàn dān chē	motorcycle
电子计算机	diàn zǐ jì suàn jī	electronic calculator
手电筒	shǒu diàn tóng	torch
无线电	wú xiàn diàn	wireless

Example:

他 喜 欢 骑 电 单 车 。
Tā xǐ huān qí diàn dān chē.
It means, "He likes riding motorcycle."

LÉI

thunder

From experience, man knows that rain clouds (雨) over his fields (田) means thunder: 雷, the voice of lightning. The original version of 雷 has three or four fields (畾) incorporated in a graphic pattern to express the reverberation of thunder. To man, thunder is impressive, but it is lightning that does the work.

"The thunder roars loudly, but little rain falls."

雷达	léi dá	radar	
雷击	léi jī	be struck by lightning	
雷鸣	léi míng	thunderous	
雷声	léi shēng	thunderclap	
雷雨	léi yǔ	thunderstorm	
雷达网	léi dá wǎng	radar service network	

雷同前人	léi tóng qián rén	mere follower of predecessors
打雷	dǎ léi	to thunder
地雷	dì léi	land-mine
水雷	shuǐ léi	sea-mine
鱼雷	yú léi	torpedo
鱼雷艇	yú léi tǐng	torpedo boat
大发雷霆	dà fā léi tíng	fly into a rage

Example:

管 工 对 工 人 大 发 雷 霆 。

Guǎn gōng duì gōng rén dà fā léi tíng.

It means, "The supervisor flies into a rage at the workers."

伞 (傘) **SǍN**
umbrella

傘 is a pictograph of an umbrella. Its radical: 人 (man) has nothing to do with the original character: 傘. Nevertheless, the regular form: 傘 seems to be harbouring four persons (众众) not included in the simplified version: 伞. Under cover of the umbrella, man counsels for the rainy day: "When the sky is clear, carry an umbrella; though your stomach is full, carry provisions."

丿 人 仌 仐 仝 伞

伞兵	sǎn bīng	paratroop; parachuter
雨伞	yǔ sǎn	umbrella
降落伞	jiàng luò sǎn	parachute

Example:

快 要 下 雨 了 ， 记 得 带 一 把 雨 伞 。
Kuài yào xià yǔ le,　jì de dài yì bǎ yǔ sǎn.

It means, "It's going to rain. Don't forget to bring an umbrella."

川 CHUĀN

river; stream

"The great river does not reject little stream." As the river meanders through arid land, infusing life into the fields, it is continually fed by little streams. Fittingly, the river is portrayed as flowing water formed by the union of little streams, upon which it vitally depends: 川 . The modern independent form: 川 uses a variant: 巛 to serve as source for other related characters.

)	)l	)ll											

川资	chuān zī	travelling expenses
川流不息	chuān liú bù xī	uninterrupted flow; continuous flow
四川	Sì Chuān	Sichuan, China

Example:

路 上 车 辆 川 流 不 息 。

Lù shàng chē liàng chuān liú bù xī.

It means, "There is a continuous flow of traffic on the road."

A mountain range, with three towering peaks, provides the structure for this pictograph of mountain or hill: 山. From a high vantage point, man is able to oversee what is easily overlooked on a lower plane. Hence the proverb: "If you don't climb the high mountain, you can't view the plain."

SHĀN

mountain;
hill

山川	shān chuān	mountains and rivers
山峰	shān fēng	summit of a mountain
山东	Shān Dōng	Shandong, China
山顶	shān dǐng	mountain top
山歌	shān gē	folk song
山谷	shān gǔ	valley
山脉	shān mài	mountain range
山坡	shān pō	hill slope
山头	shān tóu	hilltop

山西	Shān Xī	Shanxi, China
山崖	shān yá	cliff
山盟海誓	shān méng hǎi shì	solemn oath
山明水秀	shān míng shuǐ xiù	beautiful scenery
山穷水尽	shān qióng shuǐ jìn	circumstances of extreme need
山珍海味	shān zhēn hǎi wèi	delicacies

Example:

他 被 山 明 水 秀 的 西 湖 迷 住 了 。
Tā bèi shān míng shuǐ xiù de Xī Hú mí zhù le.
It means, "He was enchanted by the beautiful scenery of the West Lake."

103

鸟 (鳥) NIǍO
bird

The regular form: 鳥 is a representation of a long-tailed bird, flaunting its beauty and revelling in its freedom. Unfortunately, beauty has not always been an asset to the bird for, as the saying goes, "It's the beautiful bird that we put in the cage." Tragically, the simplified form sees the poor bird stripped of its plumage: 鸟.

| | 勹 | 勾 | 鸟 | 鸟 | | | | | | | | | |

鸟巢	niǎo cháo	bird's nest
鸟瞰	niǎo kàn	bird's eye view
鸟类	niǎo lèi	birds
鸟笼	niǎo lóng	bird cage
鸟兽	niǎo shòu	birds and animals
鸟爪	niǎo zhǎo	bird's claws

鸟语花香	niǎo yǔ huā xiāng	birds sing and flowers give forth their fragrance — characterizing a fine spring day
小鸟	xiǎo niǎo	small bird

Example:

你 家 里 有 养 鸟 吗 ?

Nǐ jiā lǐ yǒu yǎng niǎo ma ?

It means, "Do you rear birds at home?"

岛（島）

DǍO

island

Sea-birds often nest on mountainous rocks that emerge from the sea. Hence a bird (鳥) over a mountain (山) gave the concept for island: 島. The ancient form shows a bird hovering over a mountain, with feet visible: 㠀. The modern version has the bird settling on it, with feet hidden: 島, probably hatching the simplified character: 岛.

勹　勺　鸟　鸟　岛　岛

岛国	dǎo guó	island state
岛屿	dǎo yǔ	islands
半岛	bàn dǎo	peninsula
群岛	qún dǎo	archipelago

Example:

新 加 坡 是 一 个 岛 国 。
Xīn Jiā Pō shì yí gè dǎo guó.

It means, "Singapore is an island state."

乌 (鳥)

WŪ　crow

The saying: "The crow does not roost with the phoenix" sums up man's attitude towards the lowly carrion crow, regarded as a bird of ill omen. The character for crow: 乌 is similar to that for bird: 鸟, with the stroke for the eyes omitted, probably because black eyes are not readily visible against black feathers.

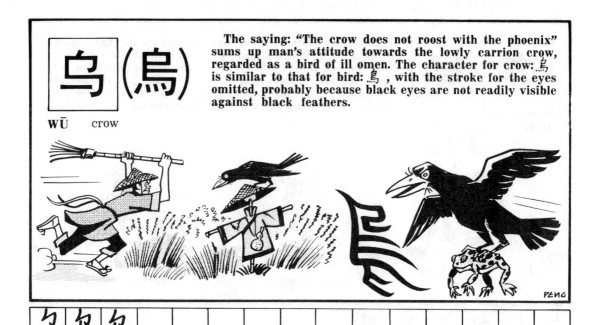

乌龟	wū guī	tortoise
乌黑	wū hēi	jet black
乌鸦	wū yā	crow
乌有	wū yǒu	naught
乌云	wū yún	dark clouds
乌贼	wū zéi	cuttlefish

乌干达	Wū Gān Dá	Uganda (Africa)
乌拉圭	Wū Lā Guī	Uruguay (Latin America)
乌托邦	Wū Tuō Bāng	Utopia
乌合之众	wū hé zhī zhòng	disorderly band
乌烟瘴气	wū yān zhàn qì	foul atmosphere

Example:

乌 龟 是 两 栖 动 物 。
Wū guī shì liǎng qī dòng wù.
It means, "The tortoise is an amphibian."

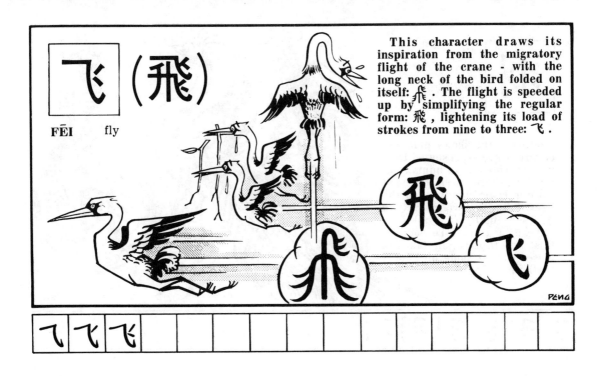

飞 （飛）

FĒI   fly

This character draws its inspiration from the migratory flight of the crane - with the long neck of the bird folded on itself: 飛. The flight is speeded up by simplifying the regular form: 飛, lightening its load of strokes from nine to three: 飞.

飞机师   fēi jī shī   pilot
飞禽走兽   fēi qín zǒu shòu   birds and beasts

Example:

他 要 做 个 飞 机 师
Tā yào zuò gè fēi jī shī.
It means, "He wants to be a pilot."

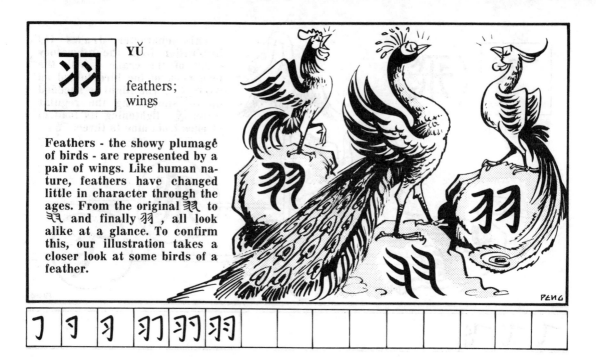

羽 YǓ

feathers; wings

Feathers - the showy plumage of birds - are represented by a pair of wings. Like human nature, feathers have changed little in character through the ages. From the original 習 to 羽 and finally 羽 , all look alike at a glance. To confirm this, our illustration takes a closer look at some birds of a feather.

羽毛	yǔ máo	feather
羽毛球	yǔ máo qiú	badminton
羽毛球拍	yǔ máo qiú pāi	badminton racket
羽毛未丰	yǔ máo wèi fēng	still young and immature

Example:

我 喜 欢 打 羽 毛 球 。
Wǒ xǐ huān dǎ yǔ máo qiú.
It means, "I like to play badminton."

108

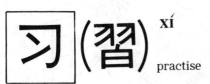

xí

practise

This ideograph combines wings (羽) with self (白, contraction of 自), suggesting a young bird learning to fly by itself; by extension, to practise: 習. Copying the bird, man also tries to fly by speeding up the simplification of the original intricate character: 習, using only one wing for "practice": 习. Woe betide the bird that copies man!

习惯	xí guàn	habit
习气	xí qì	bad habit
习俗	xí sú	custom; tradition
习题	xí tí	exercise (of school work)
习性	xí xìng	habits and characteristics
习用	xí yòng	use habitually
习语	xí yǔ	idiom

习作	xí zuò	exercises in composition, drawing, etc.
习以为常	xí yǐ wéi cháng	be used (or accustomed) to
习惯成自然	xí guàn chéng zì rán	habit becomes second nature
练习	liàn xí	practise; exercise
学习	xué xí	learning

Example:

我 们 应 该 向 伟 人 学 习 。
Wǒ men yīng gāi xiàng wěi rén xué xí.
It means, "We should learn from great men."

109

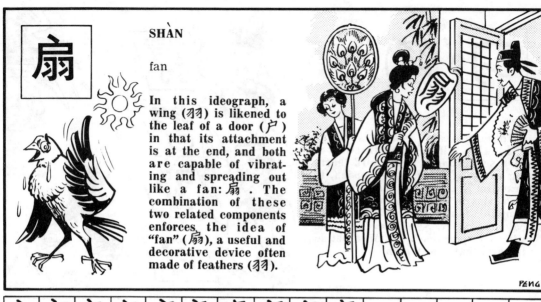

SHÀN

fan

In this ideograph, a wing (羽) is likened to the leaf of a door (户) in that its attachment is at the end, and both are capable of vibrating and spreading out like a fan: 扇 . The combination of these two related components enforces the idea of "fan" (扇), a useful and decorative device often made of feathers (羽).

丶 冫 冖 户 户 户 户 扇 扇 扇

扇动	shàn dòng	fan; flap
扇惑	shàn huò	incite; agitate
扇形	shàn xíng	fan-shaped
扇子	shàn zi	fan
一扇门	yí shàn mén	a door

Example:

这 扇 子 真 美 丽 。
Zhè shàn zi zhēng měi lì.
It means, "This is a beautiful fan."

110

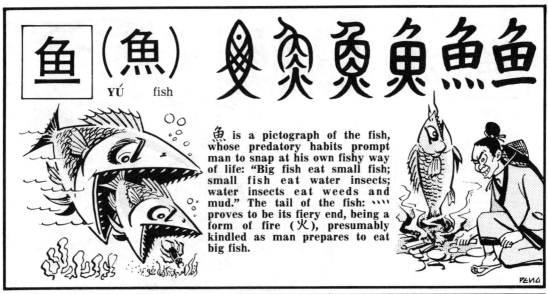

鱼 (魚)

YÚ fish

魚 is a pictograph of the fish, whose predatory habits prompt man to snap at his own fishy way of life: "Big fish eat small fish; small fish eat water insects; water insects eat weeds and mud." The tail of the fish: `````` proves to be its fiery end, being a form of fire (火), presumably kindled as man prepares to eat big fish.

鱼翅	yú chì	shark's fin (a delicacy)
鱼饵	yú ěr	fish-bait
鱼钩	yú gōu	fish-hook
鱼雷	yú léi	torpedo
鱼鳞	yú lín	fish-scales

鱼群	yú qún	shoal of fish
鱼网	yú wǎng	fishing net
鱼肝油	yú gān yóu	cod-liver oil
鱼米之乡	yú mǐ zhī xiāng	district where fish and rice are abundant

Example:

鱼 翅 是 珍 贵 的 食 品 。

Yú chì shì zhēn guì de shí pǐn.

It means, "Shark's fin is an expensive delicacy."

111

渔 (漁)

YÚ   fishing

Fish (鱼) and water (氵) are requisites for fishing (漁). The ancient form for fishing reveals water teeming with fishes: 灙. The modified form sees the number reduced to one, probably due to success in fishing: 澳. Disclosed here is yet another form of fishing - without fish or water - but it doesn't look too successful.

丶 冫 氵 氵 氵 沪 泸 泊 渔 渔 渔

渔村	yú cūn	fishing-village	渔利	yú lì	reap unfair gains
渔夫	yú fū	fisherman	渔民	yú mín	fisherman
渔港	yú gǎng	fishing port	渔业	yú yè	fishery
渔歌	yú gē	fisherman's song	渔舟	yú zhōu	fishing boat

Example:

他 是 一 个 勤 劳 的 渔 夫 。

Tā shì yī gè qín lao de yú fū.

It means, "He is a hardworking fisherman."

鲁 (魯) **LǓ**

stupid; simple

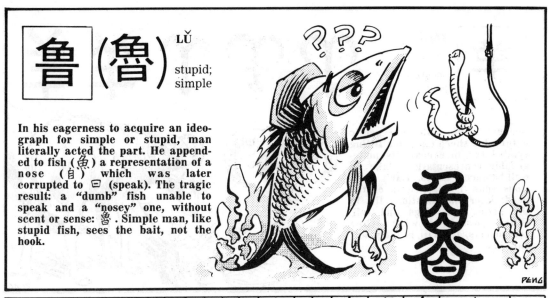

In his eagerness to acquire an ideograph for simple or stupid, man literally acted the part. He appended to fish (魚) a representation of a nose (自) which was later corrupted to 曰 (speak). The tragic result: a "dumb" fish unable to speak and a "nosey" one, without scent or sense: 魯 . Simple man, like stupid fish, sees the bait, not the hook.

| ノ | ｸ | ｸ | 乭 | 乌 | 角 | 鱼 | 鱼 | 鱼 | 鲁 | 鲁 | 鲁 | | | |

鲁钝	lǔ dùn	stupid
鲁莽	lǔ mǎng	reckless; careless

Example:

他 做 事 很 鲁 莽 。

Tā zuò shì hěn lǔ mǎng.

It means, "He does his work carelessly."

113

YÁNG

sheep; goat

Because of its mild and gentle nature, the sheep (羊) is a fitting symbol for meekness. Its pictographic representations take on well-balanced forms. Early versions show frontal views of the head; later modifications fill in the horns, ears, legs and tail. When combined with other components, the tail is often left out: 羊.

羊角	yáng jiǎo	ram's horn
羊毛	yáng máo	sheep's wool
羊排	yáng pái	mutton chop
羊皮	yáng pí	sheep skin
羊群	yáng qún	flock of sheep
羊肉	yáng ròu	mutton
羊毛衫	yáng mǎo shān	knitted sweater

羊肠小道	yáng cháng xiǎo dào	winding path
羊毛出在羊身上	yáng máo chū zài yáng shēng shàng	in the long run, you pay for whatever you are given
羔羊	gāo yáng	lamb; kid

Example:

他 不 吃 羊 肉 。

Tā bù chī yáng ròu.

It means, "He does not eat mutton."

114

鲜 (鮮)

XIĀN fresh

This character combines two types of flesh: fish (鱼) and sheep (羊). Although meat was usually preserved by salting, drying or smoking, ancient man preferred to eat the flesh of fish and sheep fresh. Hence, fish (鱼) and sheep (羊) put together means "fresh": 鲜. In other words, "flesh" becomes "fresh".

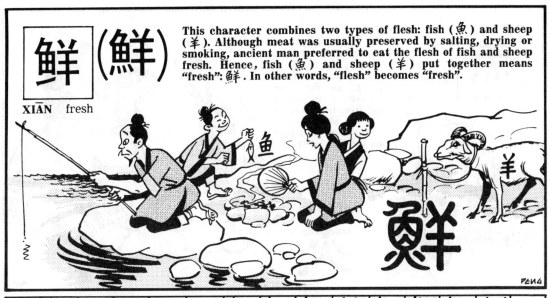

ノ	ク	ク	刍	刍	角	鱼	鱼	鱼	鱼ヽ	鱼ノ	鲜ノ	鲜ニ	鲜

鲜果	xiān guǒ	fresh fruit
鲜红	xiān hóng	bright red
鲜花	xiān huā	fresh flower
鲜美	xiān měi	delicious; tasty
鲜明	xiān míng	vividness
鲜奶	xiān nǎi	fresh milk

鲜血	xiān xuè	blood
鲜艳	xiān yàn	colourful; bright-coloured
鲜艳夺目	xiān yàn duó mù	attractive to the eyes
新鲜	xīn xiān	fresh

Example:

植 物 园 里 ， 花 儿 鲜 艳 夺 目 。

Zhí wù yuán lǐ, huā ér xiān yàn duō mù.

It means, "The flowers in the Botanic Gardens are very attractive."

115

GĀO

羔

lamb; kid

A lamb (羔) is represented by a sheep (羊) ready to stand on its feet (灬). As the four strokes (灬) stand for fire, the lamb is also a sheep (羊) ready for roasting on the fire (灬).

丶 丷 䒑 䒑 羊 羊 羊 羔 羔 羔

羔皮	gāo pí	lamb skin
羔羊	gāo yáng	kid; lamb
羔子	gāo zi	lamb; fawn

Example:

母 羊 不 见 了 羔 羊 。

Mǔ yáng bú jiàn le gāo yáng.

It means, "The ewe has lost her lamb."

MĚI

beautiful;
admirable

This beautifully proportioned character is shaped from 羊 (sheep) and 大 (big). 大 originally represented a person grown big; 羊 is an animal admired for its peace-loving virtue. Ideographically, a mature person (大) who has the mild and gentle disposition of a sheep (羊) is regarded as beautiful, admirable: 美.

丶 丷 丷 䒑 羊 羊 𦍌 羊 美

美观	měi guān	nice looking	
美国	Měi Guó	America	
美好	měi hǎo	fine; glorious	
美化	měi huà	beautify	
美景	měi jǐng	beautiful scenery	
美丽	měi lì	beautiful	
美梦	měi mèng	fond dream	
美妙	měi miào	splendid	

美满	měi mǎn	happy
美术	měi shù	fine arts
美味	měi wèi	delicious
美元	měi yuán	U.S. dollar
美联社	Měi Lián Shè	Associated Press
美容院	měi róng yuàn	beauty-parlour
美术家	měi shù jiā	artist

Example:

她 的 脸 型 很 美 。
Tā de liǎn xíng hěn měi.
It means, "She has a pretty face."

义 (義)

YÌ justice; righteousness

When justice (義) prevails, the aggressive "I": 我 (with spear 戈 in hand 手) becomes subdued like a docile and gentle sheep (羊). Hence 義 justifies itself as a symbol for right conduct. For the sake of righteousness the regular form is now slashed to three strokes, transforming it into a simplified and perfectly balanced justice: 义 .

ノ	乂	义										

义愤	yì fèn	indignation
义气	yì qì	code of brotherhood
义士	yì shì	high-minded or chivalrous person
义务	yì wù	obligation; duty

义演	yì yǎn	benefit performance
义不容辞	yì bù róng cí	be duty-bound
义务劳动	yì wù láo dòng	voluntary labour
意义	yì yì	meaning
正义	zhèng yì	justice

Example:

保 卫 国 家 是 人 民 的 义 务 。
Bǎo wèi guó jiā shì rén mín de yì wù.
It means, "It is the duty of the people to defend their own country."

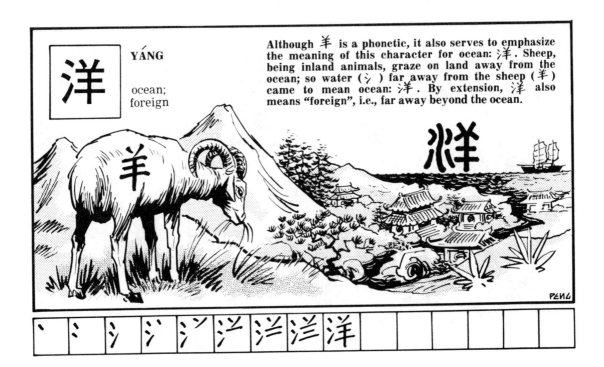

洋 YÁNG

ocean; foreign

Although 羊 is a phonetic, it also serves to emphasize the meaning of this character for ocean: 洋. Sheep, being inland animals, graze on land away from the ocean; so water (氵) far away from the sheep (羊) came to mean ocean: 洋. By extension, 洋 also means "foreign", i.e., far away beyond the ocean.

丶 丶 氵 氵 氵 氵 洋 洋 洋

洋葱	yáng cōng	onion
洋服	yáng fú	Western-style clothes
洋行	yáng háng	foreign firm
洋化	yáng huà	westernized
洋灰	yáng huī	cement
洋货	yáng huò	imported goods; foreign goods

洋人	yáng rén	foreigner
洋溢	yáng yì	fill with
洋洋得意	yáng yáng dé yì	be very pleased with oneself
海洋	hǎi yáng	ocean
大西洋	Dà Xī Yáng	Atlantic Ocean
太平洋	Tài Píng Yáng	Pacific Ocean

Example:

他 的 女 朋 友 很 洋 化 。
Tā de nǚ péng yǒu hěn yáng huà.
It means, "His girlfriend is very westernized."

This ideograph: 羨, expressive of intense desire, combines 羊 (sheep) with 次 (an old form of 涎, meaning saliva). 羨, therefore, signifies the mouth watering (次) at the sight or smell of mutton, the flesh of sheep (羊). Hence, the extended meaning: to covet or desire.

XIÀN   covet; desire

羨慕   xiàn mù   admire; envy

Example:

他 很 羨 慕 我 有 这 么 一 个 好 教 师 。
Tā hěn xiàn mù wǒ yǒu zhè me yí gè hǎo jiào shī.
It means, "He envied me for having such a good teacher."

HUǑ			
火			**火** is a pictograph of fire, produced by rubbing stones together. A terrifying force of nature, it brings both calamity and comfort to man. Like burning issues that often flare up in life, fire is easy to kindle, but difficult to handle, as the proverb warns: "You can't use paper to wrap up fire."

fire

火柴	huǒ chái	match
火车	huǒ chē	train
火光	huǒ guāng	flame; blaze
火海	huǒ hǎi	sea of fire
火花	huǒ huā	sparks
火化	huǒ huà	cremate
火箭	huǒ jiàn	rocket
火警	huǒ jǐng	fire alarm

火力	huǒ lì	fire-power
火炉	huǒ lú	furnace
火气	huǒ qì	temper
火山	huǒ shān	volcano
火星	Huǒ Xīng	Mars
火药	huǒ yào	gun-powder
火灾	huǒ zāi	fire (as a calamity)

Example:

火 车 上 人 山 人 海 。

Huǒ chē shàng rén shān rén hǎi.

It means, "The train is crowded with people."

121

炎 YÁN

blaze; flame

The character for flame (炎) itself was formed from two fires (火), one atop the other. Because of its inflammatory nature, it may well spread like wildfire and the people around it would suffer from the burning heat.

`丶` `丶丶` `丷` `火` `灭` `炏` `灻` `炎`

炎凉	yán liáng	cold-shoulder
炎热	yán rè	burning (or scorching) hot
炎夏	yán xià	hot summer
炎炎	yán yán	sweltering
炎症	yán zhèng	inflammation

Example:

今 天 天 气 很 炎 热 。

Jīn tiān tiān qì hěn yán rè.

It means, "The weather is scorching hot today."

谈 (談)

談, or words (言) beside flame (炎), aptly signifies an informal chat by the fire — idle talk in which much is spoken but little is said. Mischief arising from aimless opening of the mouth and thoughtless wagging of the tongue sparks the old saying: "Much talk brings on trouble; much food brings on indigestion."

TÁN

chat; talk

丶	讠	讠	讠	讠	谈	谈	谈	谈	谈				

谈到	tán dào	speak of
谈话	tán huà	talk; converse
谈论	tán lùn	discuss
谈判	tán pàn	negotiate
谈天	tán tiān	chit-chat

谈心	tán xīn	heart-to-heart talk
谈何容易	tán hé róng yì	easier said than done; by no means easy
谈笑风生	tán xiào fēng shēng	light-hearted and interesting talk

Example:

我 们 在 树 荫 下 谈 天 。

Wǒ men zài shù yīn xià tán tiān.

It means, "We chit-chat under the shady tree."

123

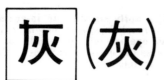

灰(灰)

HUĪ ashes; dust; lime

Fire (火) in hand (ナ) stands for ashes or dust: 灰 — the product of fire (火) that can be handled or taken in the hand (ナ). 灰 also includes lime (obtained by burning limestone) which, though easily handled (ナ), apparently contains fire (火), generating heat when mixed with water.

PENG

| 一 | 厂 | 𠂇 | 𠂇 | 灰 | 灰 | | | | | | | |

灰暗	huī àn	dim; obscure
灰尘	huī chén	dust
灰色	huī sè	grey
灰心	huī xīn	disheartened
灰心丧气	huī xīn sàng qì	downhearted

Example:

橱 上 有 一 层 灰 尘 。

Chú shàng yǒu yì céng huī chén.

It means, "There is a layer of dust on top of the cupboard."

124

灾 (災)

ZĀI calamity

Man, plagued by floods (巛, stream) and fire (火), once regarded these unforeseen calamities as divine judgement: 災. The modern simplified character for calamity: 灾, however, sets matters straight by locating fire (火) under roof (宀) — pinning the responsibility onto man himself.

丶 丷 宀 宀 宀 灾 灾

灾害	zāi hài	calamity; disaster	灾民	zāi mín	victims of natural calamity
灾患	zāi huàn	calamity	灾难	zāi nàn	misfortune
灾荒	zāi huāng	famine	灾殃	zāi yāng	catastrophe
灾祸	zāi huò	disaster	天灾	tiān zāi	natural disaster
灾情	zāi qíng	condition of a disaster	水灾	shuǐ zāi	flood
灾区	zāi qū	disaster area			

Example:

新 加 坡 很 少 发 生 水 灾 。
Xīn Jiā Pō hěn shǎo fā shēng shuǐ zāi .
It means, "Floods seldom occur in Singapore."

煽

SHĀN

incite; instigate; stir up

This ideograph literally
implies fanning (扇) a fire
(火). Figuratively, it means
to excite or incite, to
instigate or stir up: 煽 . Our
picture shows one way of
fanning a flame, in line with
the proverb: "Fuel alone will
not ignite a fire".

丶 丷 少 火 火 灯 灯 炉 炉 炉 煸 煽 煽 煽

煽动	shān dòng	instigate; incite
煽乱	shān luàn	stir up revolt
煽动者	shān dòng zhě	agitator
煽风点火	shān fēng diǎn huǒ	create trouble

Example:

他 煽 动 旧 同 学 欺 侮 新 同 学 。

Tā shān dòng jiù tóng xué qī wǔ xīn tóng xué

It means, "He instigated his classmates to bully the new student."

126

烧 (燒)

SHĀO burn; bake; roast

燒 probably originated from the firing (火) of earthenware (圭) stacked upon a support (兀) in a kiln. The phonetic: 堯, showing earth (圭) piled up high on a pedestal (兀) denotes high or great. Combination with the radical: 火 (fire) generates the character: 燒 which stands for the great heat required in baking, roasting or burning: 燒.

丶　丷　少　火　灯　灶　灶　烧　烧　烧

烧毁	shāo huǐ	destroy by fire	烧死	shāo sǐ	be burnt to death
烧火	shāo huǒ	make a fire	烧香	shāo xiāng	incense-offering
烧焦	shāo jiāo	scorch	烧窑	shāo yáo	kiln
烧肉	shāo ròu	roast meat	发烧	fā shāo	fever
烧伤	shāo shāng	injury from burns			

Example:

她 常 去 寺 庙 烧 香 。

Tā cháng qù sì miào shāo xiāng.

It means, "She often goes to the temple to offer incense."

HEĪ

black

The original seal form depicted a flame (炎) under a smoke vent or window (⊕), blackening it (쬤) with soot. Squaring the window: 田 and modifying the flame: 杰, produced the modern character: 黑, meaning black.

黑暗	heī′ àn	dark	黑心	heī xīn	black-hearted; evil-minded
黑白	heī bái	black and white			
黑板	heī bǎn	blackboard	黑夜	heī yè	dark night
黑人	heī rén	Black people	黑名单	heī míng dān	blacklist
黑色	heī sè	black	黑啤酒	heī pí jiǔ	stout
黑市	heī shì	black market	乌黑	wū heī	jet black

Example:

她 怕 黑 暗 。

Tā pà heī àn

It means, "She is afraid of the dark."

MÒ

墨 ink;
Chinese ink

Chinese ink: 墨 was first made by mixing smoke-soot (黑) with gum to produce an earthy (土) substance. The mixture was then moulded and hardened into a solid stick, ready to be ground with water to form live ink. Even though a little ink is better than a good memory, man apparently prefers to heed the proverb: "He who is near ink gets black," committing it to memory.

丶 冂 冂 冂 四 四 罕 罤 罤 罼 黑 黑 黑 黑 墨

墨迹	mò jī	ink mark
墨水	mò shuǐ	ink
墨砚	mò yàn	inkstone
墨鱼	mò yú	inkfish; cuttlefish

| 墨汁 | mò zhī | prepared Chinese ink |
| 墨水笔 | mò shuǐ bǐ | fountain pen |

Example:

我 喜 欢 用 墨 水 笔 写 字 。
Wǒ xǐ huān yòng mò shuǐ bǐ xiě zì.
It means, "I like to write with a fountain pen."

点 (點)

DIĂN point; spot; dot

The phonetic component: 占 means to divine, to ask about or interpret orally (口) the cracks (卜) of a heated tortoise shell — to point out the unknown. Adding the radical component: 黑 (black) emphasizes the point with black. Hence: 點 , a black point, a spot or dot. The simplified version comes even more to the point: 点 by setting divination (占) on fire (灬).

| 卜 | 卜 | 卜 | 占 | 占 | 占 | 点 | 点 | 点 | | | | | |

点菜	diǎn cài	choose dishes from a menu		
点滴	diǎn dī	droplet		
点火	diǎn huǒ	light a fire		
点名	diǎn míng	call the roll		

点燃	diǎn rán	kindle
点头	diǎn tóu	nod one's head
点心	diǎn xīn	light refreshments
点缀	diǎn zhuì	decorate

Example:

他 把 蜡 烛 点 燃 了 。
Tā bǎ là zhú diǎn rán le.
It means, "He lighted the candle."

130

CǍO

草

grass; weeds

屮屮 is a pictograph of grass, commonly written: 草. The contracted form is 艹. Despised as weed that sways with the wind, the lowly grass (艹) nevertheless provides the root for a host of "plant" characters. And, unlike the grassroots of human society, it can draw comfort from the proverb: "Every blade of grass has its own share of dew."

一 十 艹 艹 芒 苫 苗 莒 草

草包	cǎo bāo	block-head; good-for-nothing	草莓	cǎo méi	strawberry
草草	cǎo cǎo	done rashly	草皮	cǎo pí	turf; sod
草稿	cǎo gǎo	manuscript; draft	草率	cǎo shuài	careless
草菇	cǎo gū	straw mushroom	草席	cǎo xí	straw mat
草绿	cǎo lǜ	grass green	草药	cǎo yào	medicinal herb
草帽	cǎo mào	straw hat	草原	cǎo yuán	grasslands

Example:

马 儿 爱 吃 草 。

Mǎr ài chī cǎo.

It means, "Horses like to eat grass."

131

苗

MIÁO

sprouts;
shoots

THE concept of "sprout" (苗) germinates from grain stalks (艹) sprouting in a cultivated field (田). By extension, 苗 includes man's offspring, his progeny. As illustration, we picture here a productive farmer with his "sprouts" — the fruit of much labour of love and toil.

一 十 艹 艻 苧 苩 苗 苗

苗条	miáo tiáo	slender and slim
苗族	miáo zú	the Miao tribe
树苗	shù miáo	sapling
幼苗	yòu miáo	seedling

Example:

那 位 小 姐 的 身 材 很 苗 条 。
Nà wèi xiǎo jiě de shēn cái hěn miáo tiáo.

It means, "That lady has a slender and slim figure."

132

叶 (葉) YÈ

leaves

THE seal form: 枼 graphically portrays the luxuriant foliage of a tree. The regular form: 葉, signifying the generations (世) of a treelike (木) plant (艹), suggests the seasonal sprouting of leaves. The simplified form, however, simply borrows the character: 叶 (originally "harmony") and leaves the harmonizing to the imagination.

丨	冂	口	口-	叶										

叶柄	yè bǐng	leafstalk
叶子	yè zi	leaf
叶落归根	yè luò guī gēn	falling leaves settle on their roots—a person residing elsewhere finally returns to his ancestral home
枫叶	fēng yè	maple leaf

Example:

这 片 叶 子 好 大 啊 ！
Zhè piàn yè zǐ hǎo dà à ！
It means, "What a big leaf!"

HUĀ

花

flowers

ORIGINALLY, 化 pictured a man tumbling heels over head, indicating a complete change — a metamorphosis. With the plant radical (艹) grafted on, 化 assumed a different character and blossomed into a flower: 花 — that part of a plant (艹) which is strikingly transformed (化) or changed from the other parts.

一 十 艹 艹 艻 芢 花 花

花瓣	huā bàn	petal
花边	huā biān	lace
花草	huā cǎo	flowers and plants
花朵	huā duǒ	flower
花篮	huā lán	flower basket
花瓶	huā píng	vase
花圈	huā quān	wreath
花生	huā shēng	peanut
花园	huā yuán	garden

花生米	huā shēng mǐ	shelled peanut
花花公子	huā huā gōng zǐ	dandy; coxcomb; fop
花花绿绿	huā huā lǜ lǜ	colourful
花花世界	huā huā shì jiè	the dazzling human world with its myriad temptations; this mortal world

Example:

这 朵 花 儿 很 美 丽 。

Zhè duǒ huā ér hěn měi lì.

It means, "This flower is very beautiful."

134

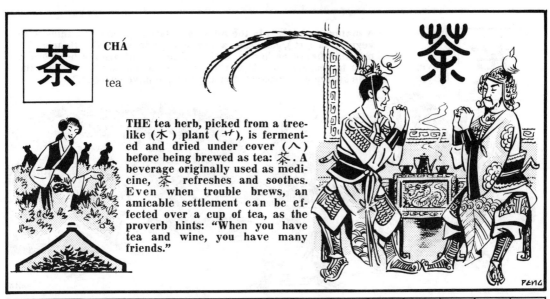

茶

CHÁ

tea

THE tea herb, picked from a tree-like (木) plant (艹), is fermented and dried under cover (人) before being brewed as tea: 茶. A beverage originally used as medicine, 茶 refreshes and soothes. Even when trouble brews, an amicable settlement can be effected over a cup of tea, as the proverb hints: "When you have tea and wine, you have many friends."

一 十 艹 艹 艾 苂 苂 茶 茶

茶杯	chá bēi	teacup	
茶匙	chá chí	teaspoon	
茶点	chá diǎn	refreshments	
茶巾	chá jīn	tea cloth	
茶具	chá jù	tea-set	
茶壶	chá hú	teapot	
茶会	chá huì	tea-party	

茶钱	chá qián	tip
茶水	chá shuǐ	tea or boiled water
茶叶	chá yè	tea-leaves
茶座	chá zuò	tea-house
茶园	chá yuán	tea plantation
喝茶	hē chá	drink tea

Example:

我 喜 欢 喝 茶 。

Wǒ xǐ huān hē chá .

It means, "I like to drink tea."

英 YĪNG
brave; heroic

A mature man (大) in the midst of a large space (宀), thick with vegetation (艹), suggests a brave man in a jungle. Hence: 英, meaning brave or heroic. Although there will always be a brave man to respond to a high reward, the ancient saying reveals the true source of courage: "Men of principle have courage."

一 十 艹 艹 节 苫 英 英

英镑	yīng bàng	pound sterling	
英才	yīng cái	person of out-standing ability	
英国	Yīng Guó	England	
英豪	yīng háo	hero	
英俊	yīng jùn	handsome	
英明	yīng míng	brilliant	
英名	yīng míng	illustrious name	
英文	yīng wén	English (language)	

英雄	yīng xióng	hero
英勇	yīng yǒng	courageous
英语	yīng yǔ	English (language)
英姿	yīng zī	valiant and fine-looking
英国人	yīng guó rén	Englishman
英联邦	yīng lián bāng	British Commonwealth (of Nations)

Example:

岳 飞 是 宋 朝 的 一 位 英 雄 人 物 。

Yuè Fēi shì Sòng cháo de yí wèi yīng xióng rén wù.

It means, "Yue Fei was a heroic figure of the Song dynasty."

竹 ZHÚ

bamboo

ORIGINALLY written: 个个, the character for bamboo is a pictograph of two whorls of bamboo leaves. Unlike a wayward man, the bamboo grows straight and upright into a useful and decorative plant. "The bamboo stick makes a good child," so says the proverb. Our picture demonstrates how — starting right from the bottom.

ノ	ト	个	竹	竹	竹

竹竿	zhú gān	bamboo pole
竹林	zhú lín	bamboo grove
竹荀	zhú sǔn	bamboo shoot
竹子	zhú zi	bamboo

竹叶青	zhú yè qīng	bamboo-leaf-green liqueur
山竹	shān zhú	mangosteen

Example:

这 椅 子 是 竹 做 的 。
Zhè yǐ zi shì zhú zuò de.

It means, "This chair is made of bamboo."

137

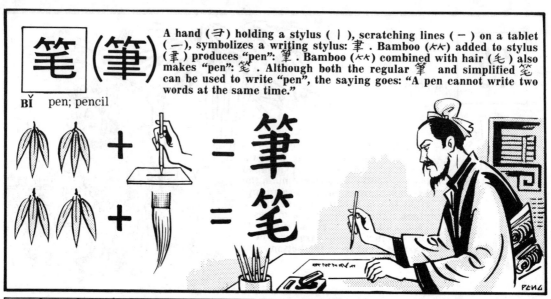

笔 (筆)

BǏ pen; pencil

A hand (⺕) holding a stylus (丨), scratching lines (一) on a tablet (一), symbolizes a writing stylus: 聿 . Bamboo (⺮) added to stylus (聿) produces "pen": 筆 . Bamboo (⺮) combined with hair (毛) also makes "pen": 笔 . Although both the regular 筆 and simplified 笔 can be used to write "pen", the saying goes: "A pen cannot write two words at the same time."

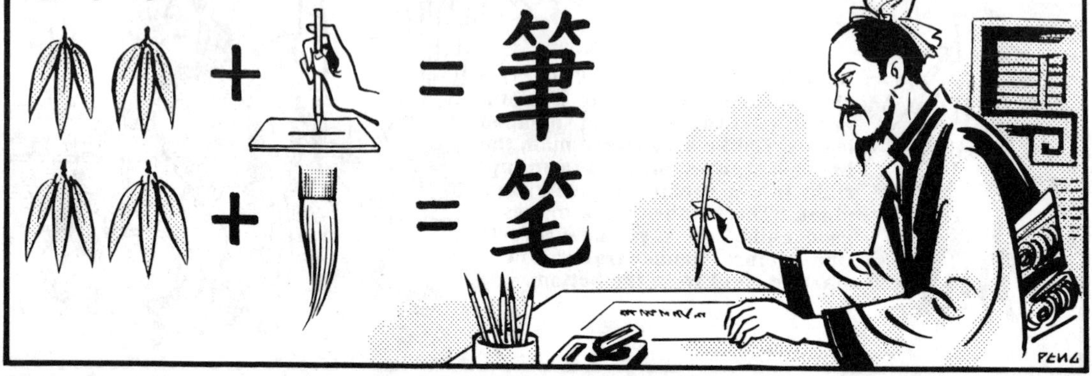

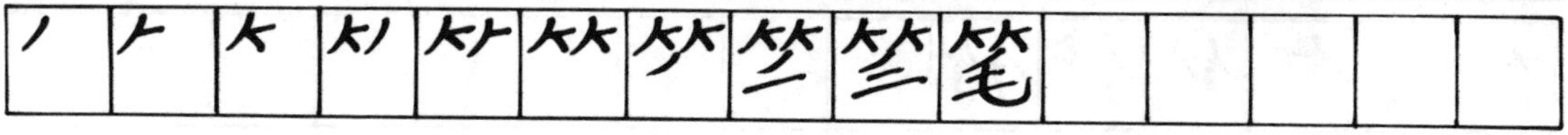

笔调	bǐ diào	(of writing) tone	笔名	bǐ míng	pseudonym
笔法	bǐ fǎ	technique of writing	笔墨	bǐ mò	pen and ink
笔画	bǐ huà	strokes of a Chinese character	笔试	bǐ shì	written examination
笔记	bǐ jì	notes	笔误	bǐ wù	slip of the pen
笔迹	bǐ jì	writing	笔战	bǐ zhàn	written polemics
笔尖	bǐ jiān	pen nib	钢笔	gāng bǐ	fountain pen
			铅笔	qiān bǐ	pencil

Example:

他 的 笔 迹 很 美 。

Tā de bǐ jì hěn měi.

It means, "He has beautiful handwriting."

算 **SUÀN**

calculate; plan

算, the character for calculate or plan, is cleverly conceived: two hands (廾) manipulating an abacus (目) made of bamboo (𥫗). Although 算 emphasizes doing with the hands, it also means to contrive, as exemplified by the character shown here who is planning more and doing less.

ノ　ㅏ　⺊　⺮　⺮　竹　竹　竹　筲　筲　筲　算　算

算法	suàn fǎ	algorithm	算术	suàn shù	arithmetic
算命	suàn mìng	fortune-telling	计算	jì suàn	calculate
算盘	suàn pān	abacus			

Example:

他 的 算 术 是 班 上 最 好 的 。

Tā de suàn shù shì bān shàng zuì hǎo de.

It means, "He tops the class in arithmetic."

XIÀO

笑

laugh; smile

笑 has an amusing origin. The phonetic element: 夭 depicts a man (大) inclining his head (丿) to laugh more easily, suggesting rocking or shaking. The radical component: ⺮ likens such laughter to the swaying of bamboo (⺮) in the breeze. But laughing or smiling is serious business, as implied in the proverb: "A man without a smiling face should not open a shop."

| ノ | ⺊ | ⺮ | ⺮丨 | ⺮丨 | 𝘬𝘬 | 𝘬𝘬 | 𝘬𝘬 | 笊 | 笑 | | | | | |

笑柄	xiào bǐng	laughing-stock	
笑话	xiào huà	joke	
笑剧	xiào jù	farce	
笑脸	xiào liǎn	smiling face	
笑料	xiào liào	laughing-stock	
笑骂	xiào mà	deride and taunt	
笑容	xiào róng	smiling expression	
笑哈哈	xiào hā hā	laughingly	
笑面虎	xiào miàn hǔ	smiling tiger	

笑嘻嘻	xiào xī xī	grinning
笑里藏刀	xiào lǐ cáng dāo	hide a dagger in a smile; (figuratively) with murderous intent behind one's smile
笑脸常开	xiào liǎn cháng kāi	put on a smiling face always
笑逐颜开	xiào zhú yán kāi	beam with smiles

Example:

他 喜 欢 讲 笑 话 。
Tā xǐ huān jiǎng xiào huà.

It means, "He likes to joke."

禾 HÉ

grain

禾, the radical for "grain", is a tree (木) with the top bent over to represent the head of a ripened grain. The grain-stalk provides, not only food for the body, but also food for thought: the more grain it bears in the head, the more it bends in humility.

ノ 一 千 千 禾

禾叉	hé chā	pitchfork	禾黍	hé shǔ	millet
禾虫	hé chóng	harvest grub	禾穗	hé suì	a ear (of rice grain)
禾苗	hé miáo	grain seedling			

Example:

禾 苗 已 经 长 大 了 。

Hé miáo yǐ jīng zhǎng dà le.

It means, "The grain seedlings have fully grown."

141

QIŪ

秋 autumn

During the autumn harvest, the grain (禾) ripens under the fiery heat (火) of the sun. Hence: 秋 , meaning "autumn". In China, one can see the waste stalks of grain (禾) disposed of by fire (火) after the harvesting and threshing in Autumn.

ノ 二 千 矛 禾 禾 禾ノ 秒 秋

秋波	qiū bō	bright eyes of a beautiful woman	秋水	qiū shuǐ	autumn waters
秋季	qiū jì	autumn season	秋天	qiū tiān	autumn
秋千	qiū qiān	swing	秋种	qiū zhòng	autumn sowing
秋色	qiū sè	autumn scenery	春秋时代	Chūn Qiū Shí Dài	The Spring and Autumn period (B.C. 722-481) in Chinese history
秋收	qiū shōu	autumn harvest			

Example:

秋 天 的 景 色 很 美 。

Qiū tiān de jǐng sè hěn měi .

It means, "The scenery in autumn is beautiful."

CHÓU

sad; melancholy

As the year declines, with each falling leaf signalling autumn (秋), man's heart (心) becomes weighed down with a nostalgic melancholy: 愁. He realizes nature cannot jump from winter to summer without a spring or from summer to winter without a fall. Hence: 愁 — the influence of autumn (秋) on the heart (心).

PENG

丿 二 千 千 禾 禾 禾丿 利丿 秋 秋 愁 愁 愁

愁肠	chóu cháng	pent-up feelings of sadness		愁容	chóu róng	sorrowful countenance
愁苦	chóu kǔ	anxiety; distress		愁绪	chóu xù	gloomy mood
愁眉	chóu méi	knitted brows		愁眉苦脸	chóu méi kǔ liǎn	distressed look
愁闷	chóu mèn	feel gloomy				

Example:

她 的 脸 充 满 愁 容 。

Tā de liǎn chōng mǎn chóu róng.

It means, "She looks sorrowful."

143

SHUÌ

税

tax

To justify taxation, man coined 税 from 禾 (grain) and 兑 (exchange). Evidently farmers paid their taxes in grain (禾) in "exchange" (兑) for services and privileges. The proverb, however, has the last word: "Those who are prospering do not argue about taxes." They just close their eyes, shut their mouths and pay through the nose.

ノ 二 手 矛 矛 禾 利 利 税 税 秒 税

税额	shuì é	amount of tax to be paid
税款	shuì kuǎn	tax payment; taxation
税率	shuì lǜ	tax rate

税收	shuì shōu	tax revenue
税制	shuì zhì	tax system
税务局	shuì wù jú	tax bureau
税务员	shuì wù yuān	tax collector

Example:

我 已 经 付 了 所 得 税 。
Wǒ yǐ jīng fù le suǒ dé shuì.
It means, "I have paid my income tax."

144

禿

TŪ   bald; bare

This ideograph likens the top or head of man (几) to a field of grain (禾) after the harvest. Hence: 禿, meaning bare or bald. We show here man in the autumn of his life — after his very last harvest.

丿 亻 千 禾 禾 禾 禿

禿笔	tū bǐ	bald writing brush—(figuratively) poor writing ability	
禿顶	tū dǐng	bald	
禿山	tū shān	barren hill	

禿头	tū tóu	bald head
禿子	tū zi	baldhead
光禿禿	guāng tū tū	bare; bald

Example:

他 的 头 光 禿 禿 。

Tā de tóu guāng tū tū.

It means, "His head is bald."

145

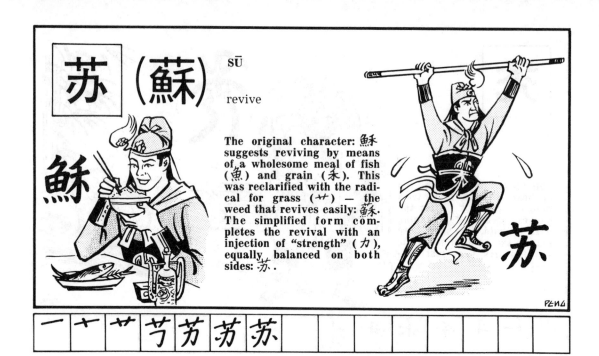

苏（蘇）

SŪ

revive

The original character: 穌 suggests reviving by means of a wholesome meal of fish (魚) and grain (禾). This was reclarified with the radical for grass (艹) — the weed that revives easily: 蘇. The simplified form completes the revival with an injection of "strength" (力), equally balanced on both sides: 苏.

一　十　艹　艻　芀　苏　苏

苏打	sū dá	soda	苏醒	sū xǐng	revive; regain consciousness
苏丹	Sū Dān	Sultan; Sudan (in Africa)	苏州	Sū Zhōu	Suzhou (Soochow), China
苏联	Sū Lián	Soviet Union	苏格兰	Sū Gé Lán	Scotland
苏息	sū xí	rest			

Example:

她 苏 醒 过 来 了 。

Tā sū xǐng guò lái le.

It means, "She has regained consciousness."

146

HÉ

harmony; and

Grain (禾), being man's staple food, is most agreeable to the mouth (口). Hence, grain (禾) agrees with mouth (口) to produce harmony: 和. Also agreeable is the proverbial saying: "If a family lives in harmony, all affairs will prosper."

ノ 二 千 千 禾 利 和 和

和蔼	hé ǎi	amiable	
和风	hé fēng	gentle breeze	
和服	hé fú	kimono	
和缓	hé huǎn	gentle; mild	
和会	hé huì	peace conference	
和解	hé jiě	become reconciled	
和局	hé jú	drawn game; tie	
和暖	hé nuǎn	pleasantly warm	
和平	hé píng	peace	

和气	hé qì	friendly
和尚	hé shàng	Buddhist monk
和约	hé yuē	peace treaty
和平共处	hé píng gòng chǔ	peaceful co-existence
和颜悦色	hé yán yuè sè	benign countenance or amiable manner
和睦相处	hé mù xiāng chǔ	live harmoniously

Example:

同 学 们 和 睦 相 处 ！
Tóng xué men hé mù xiāng chǔ.
It means, "The students live harmoniously."

NIÁN

year

"Flowers bloom year by year with the same beauty, but man changes from year to year." Man's fickleness is evident in his quest for a suitable character for "year".

The original pictograph: 夫 showed a man bearing a sheaf of grains — the job of the year.

This was replaced by an ideograph: 秊 , combining 千 (thousand) and 禾 (grain), i.e., the thousand stalks — the harvest of a year.

Then came 秊 , based on the radical: 干 (shield), followed by the contraction: 年 . Figuring these out would be quite a task — the work of a year.

丿	亠	乍	乍	乍	年										

年报	nián bào	annual report
年初	nián chū	beginning of a year
年代	nián dài	age; years; era
年底	nián dǐ	end of a year
年度	nián dù	year
年份	nián fèn	particular year
年糕	nián gāo	New Year cake made of glutinous rice flour

年关	nián guān	end of a year
年龄	nián líng	age
年迈	nián mài	aged
年年	nián nián	every year
年轻	nián qīng	young
年夜	nián yè	eve of the lunar New Year
成年	chéng nián	adult; all year round
新年	xīn nián	New Year

Example:

我 很 喜 欢 吃 年 糕 。

Wǒ hěn xǐ huān chī nián gāo.

It means, "I like to eat New Year cake."

甘 GĀN

sweet

"Sweetness" is handled with taste in the proverb: "All food tastes sweet to those who are hungry." The radical for "sweet" pictures the mouth (口) with something (一) in it worth holding — something sweet: 甘 . 甘 can be extended to include anything pleasing to the senses, as illustrated here.

| 一 | 十 | 廿 | 廿 | 甘 | | | | | | | |

甘草	gān cǎo	licorice root
甘苦	gān kǔ	weal and woe
甘露	gān lù	sweet dew
甘美	gān měi	sweet and refreshing
甘心	gān xīn	willingly; readily

甘愿	gān yuàn	readily
甘蔗	gān zhe	sugarcane
甘心情愿	gān xīn qíng yuàn	willingly and gladly
苦尽甘来	kǔ jìn gān lái	after suffering comes happiness

Example:

我 喜 欢 喝 甘 蔗 汁 。

Wǒ xǐ huān hē gān zhè zhī.

It means, "I like to drink sugarcane juice."

149

XIĀNG

fragrant

The seal form of this radical for fragrance represents the sweet (甘) odour of millet (黍) undergoing fermentation: 香. Grain (禾), the essence of millet grain (黍), was distilled for the modified version: 香, leading to the modern form: 香.

丿	二	千	千	禾	禾	香	香	香

香肠	xiāng cháng	sausage	香气	xiāng qì	aroma
香菜	xiāng cài	coriander	香水	xiāng shuǐ	perfume
香粉	xiāng fěn	face powder	香味	xiāng wèi	sweet smell
香菇	xiāng gū	mushroom	香烟	xiāng yān	cigarette
香花	xiāng huā	fragrant flower	香皂	xiāng zào	soap
香蕉	xiāng jiāo	banana	香槟酒	xiāng bīn jiǔ	champagne
香料	xiāng liào	spice	香喷喷	xiāng pēn pēn	sweet-smelling

Example:

这 朵 花 好 香 啊 !

Zhè duǒ huā hǎo xiāng a !

It means, "What a sweet-scented flower!"

150

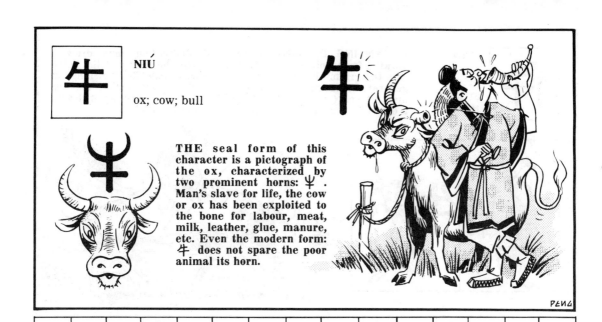

牛 NIÚ

ox; cow; bull

THE seal form of this character is a pictograph of the ox, characterized by two prominent horns: Ψ. Man's slave for life, the cow or ox has been exploited to the bone for labour, meat, milk, leather, glue, manure, etc. Even the modern form: 牛 does not spare the poor animal its horn.

ノ 乂 仁 牛

牛痘	niú dòu	cowpox	牛棚	niú péng	cowshed
牛角	niú jiǎo	ox-horn	牛脾气	niú pí qi	stubbornness; obstinacy
牛劲	niú jìn	great strength			
牛马	niú mǎ	oxen and horses — beasts of burden	牛肉	niú ròu	beef
			牛尾	niú wěi	oxtail
牛奶	niú nǎi	milk	牛仔裤	niú zǎi kù	jeans
牛排	niú pái	beef steak			

Example:

多 喝 牛 奶 对 身 体 有 益 。

Duō hē niú nǎi duì shēn tǐ yǒu yì.

It means, "Milk is good for the health."

151

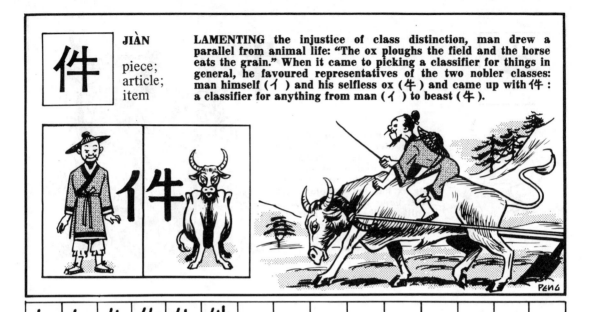

JIÀN

件

piece;
article;
item

LAMENTING the injustice of class distinction, man drew a parallel from animal life: "The ox ploughs the field and the horse eats the grain." When it came to picking a classifier for things in general, he favoured representatives of the two nobler classes: man himself (亻) and his selfless ox (牛) and came up with 件: a classifier for anything from man (亻) to beast (牛).

ノ 亻 亻 仁 仵 件

案件	àn jiàn	legal case	文件	wén jiàn	document
密件	mì jiàn	confidential document	一件行李	yī jiàn xíng lǐ	piece of luggage
事件	shì jiàn	matter; event; affair			

Example:

他 的 抽 屉 里 有 很 多 机 密 文 件 。

Tā de chōu tì lǐ yǒu hěn duō jī mì wén jiàn.

It means, "There are many confidential documents in his drawer."

152

LÁO

牢

cattle pen;
prison

THE seal form; 牢 pictures a paddock (𝛀) confining an ox (牛) after the day's hard labour. The modern form: 牢 mercifully puts a roof (宀) over the beast (牛). By extension, 牢 represents a prison for the incarceration of "beasts" of human society who are also in for "hard labour".

PENG

丶 丷 宀 宀 宀 牢 牢

牢固	láo gù	firm; secure
牢记	láo jì	remember well
牢牢	láo láo	firmly; safely
牢骚	láo sāo	grumbling; complaint

牢狱; 监牢	láo yù; jiān láo	prison; jail
牢不可破	láo bù kě pò	unbreakable
坐牢	zuò láo	be in prison

Example:

他 因 犯 罪 而 被 判 坐 牢 。
Tā yīn fàn zuì ér bèi pàn zuò láo.
It means, "He was sentenced to jail."

153

BÀN

half

THIS character originated from the butcher's practice of dividing (八) an ox (牛) into two halves, in all its length, before cutting up. 牛 was modified to 牛 to facilitate exact division. Hence: 半, meaning "half". Even though it is easy to split one ox into two halves, the saying proves true: "You cannot get two skins from one ox."

ヽ　ソ　ソ　半　半

半边	bàn biān	one side (of something)
半岛	bàn dǎo	peninsula
半价	bàn jià	half-price
半票	bàn piào	half-price ticket
半生	bàn shēng	half a lifetime
半数	bàn shù	half the number
半天	bàn tiān	half of the day

半途	bàn tú	halfway
半夜	bàn yè	midnight
半官方	bàn guān fāng	semi-official
半决赛	bàn jué sài	semi-finals
半斤八两	bàn jīn bā liǎng	not much to choose between the two
半途而废	bàn tú ér fèi	give up halfway

Example:

他 做 事 总 是 半 途 而 废 。
Tā zuò shì zǒng shì bàn tú ér fèi.

It means, "He always gives up his work halfway."

154

BÀN

companion;
associate;
mate

THE ideograph: 伴 is made up of man (亻) and half (半), suggesting that the single man is but half of a pair. To attain "oneness" another half, a complement, is needed. Hence: 伴 , meaning companion, associate or mate. In the choice of a better half, let man take heed: "Tiger and deer do not walk together."

丿 亻 亻 伵 伴 伴 伴

伴唱	bàn chàng	vocal accompani-ment	
伴侣	bàn lǚ	companion; partner	
伴娘	bàn niáng	bridesmaid; maid-of-honour	

伴随	bàn suí	accompany; follow
伴奏	bàn zòu	accompany with musical instru-ments
做伴	zuō bàn	keep somebody company

Example:

她 唱 歌 时 需 要 有 人 伴 奏 。
Tā chàng gē shí xū yào yǒu rén bàn zòu.
It means, "Whenever she sings, she needs instrumental accompaniment."

GÀO

indict;
tell;
inform

ORIGINALLY 告 means to indict or accuse, i.e., do with the mouth (口) what the ox (牛) does with the horns: to gore. By extension it also means to tell, inform or even to warn. So, before starting to gore like an ox, be warned: "Man knows not his own fault; the ox knows not its strength."

告别	gào bié	bid farewell to
告吹	gào chuī	fizzle out; fail
告辞	gào cí	take leave (of one's host)
告发	gào fā	report an offence
告假	gào jià	ask for leave
告示	gào shì	official notice
告诉	gào sù	tell
自告奋勇	zì gào fèn yǒng	volunteer to do something

告退	gào tuì	ask for leave to withdraw from a meeting
告知	gào zhī	inform
告状	gào zhuàng	lodge complaint; bring a suit against
警告	jǐng gào	warning
不告而别	bù gào ér bié	leaving without saying goodbye

Example:

请 你 告 诉 我 怎 样 去 植 物 园 ?
Qǐng nǐ gào sù wǒ zěn yàng qù Zhí Wù Yuán ?
It means, "Will you please tell me the way to the Botanic Gardens?"

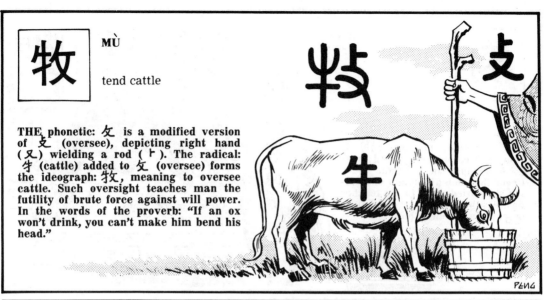

牧 **MÙ**

tend cattle

THE phonetic: 攴 is a modified version of 支 (oversee), depicting right hand (又) wielding a rod (卜). The radical: 牛 (cattle) added to 攴 (oversee) forms the ideograph: 牧, meaning to oversee cattle. Such oversight teaches man the futility of brute force against will power. In the words of the proverb: "If an ox won't drink, you can't make him bend his head."

丿 ㄠ 牛 牜 牜 牧 牧 牧

牧草	mù cǎo	forage grass	
牧场	mù chǎng	grazing land	
牧放	mù fàng	tend; herd	
牧歌	mù gē	pastoral song	
牧民	mù mín	herdsman	
牧区	mù qū	pastoral area	

牧师	mù shī	pastor; clergyman
牧童	mù tóng	shepherd boy
牧业	mù yè	animal husbandry
牧羊人	mù yáng rén	shepherd
游牧生活	yóu mù shēng huó	nomadic life

Example:

牧 童 在 草 原 上 牧 羊 。

Mù tóng zài cǎo yuán shàng mù yáng.

It means, "The shepherd boy is tending sheep on the plain."

157

ROU

flesh; meat

THE character for meat: 肉 is composed of pieces of dried meat (仌) wrapped in a bundle (冂). From the ancient custom of offering such dried meat to the teacher came the term: "dried-meat money" - a teacher's pay.

肉饼	ròu bǐng	meat pie
肉搏	ròu bó	fight hand-to-hand
肉店	ròu diàn	butcher's (shop)
肉干	ròu gān	barbequed meat
肉麻	ròu má	nauseating; disgusting
肉排	ròu pái	steak
肉片	ròu piàn	sliced meat

肉体	ròu tǐ	human body
肉丸	ròu wán	meatball
肉刑	ròu xíng	corporal punishment
牛肉	niú ròu	beef
羊肉	yáng ròu	mutton
猪肉	zhū ròu	pork

Example:

马 来 人 不 吃 猪 肉 。
Mǎ lái rén bù chī zhū ròu .

It means, "The Malays do not eat pork."

胖 PÀNG

fat; fleshy

THE original idea of 半 is "half a bull", denoting size. The radical: 月 (flesh) supplements the thought, indicating fleshiness. Hence 胖 : fleshy or fat. Beefiness and other bovine characteristics are not altogether undesirable according to the proverb: "You win a cat and lose a cow."

丿	刀	月	月	月	月	肝	肝	胖					

胖子　　　pàng zi　　　fat person
发胖　　　fā pàng　　　put on weight

Example:

他 胖 起 来 了 。
Tā pàng qǐ lái le.

It means, "He is putting on weight."

159

YǑU

have

EARLY forms portrayed a hand (ㄆ) grasping a piece of meat (𠕎), signifying to possess or to have: 𠂇. Because of the resemblance between meat (𠕎) and moon (𠕎), man soon lost sight of meat and reached for the moon, promising it to anyone he wishes to possess. Today, with hand (𠂇) on moon (月), he classified 有 under "moon".

PENG

一 ナ 才 冇 有 有

有功	yǒu gōng	have rendered great service
有关	yǒu guān	related to; have something to do with
有害	yǒu hài	harmful; detrimental
有理	yǒu lǐ	reasonable
有利	yǒu lì	advantageous; favourable

有力	yǒu lì	strong; powerful
有效	yǒu xiào	efficacious; valid
有机可乘	yǒu jī kě chéng	there's an opportunity to take advantage of
有利可图	yǒu lì kě tú	stand to gain
有目共睹	yǒu mù gòng dǔ	be there for all to see
有求必应	yǒu qiú bì yìng	respond to every plea

Example:

我 没 有 汽 车 。
Wǒ méi yǒu qì chē.

It means, "I don't have a car."

来 (來) LÁI

come

"HE who sows his grain in the field puts his trust in heaven," so observed the proverb. A bountiful yield of grain was therefore gratefully acknowledged as having "come" from above. Thus 來, originally a pictograph of growing wheat or barley, came to stand for "come". The simplified form grafts rice (米) on to tree (木) to produce 来 — a character no less welcome.

一　厂　斤　三　丰　夬　来

来宾	lái bīn	guest	
来到	lái dào	arrive; come	
来电	lái diàn	incoming telegram	
来访	lái fǎng	come to visit	
来回	lái huí	make a round trip	
来件	lái jiàn	communication or parcel received	
来客	lái kè	guest	
来临	lái lín	approach; come	

来年	lái nián	next year	
来生	lái shēng	next life	
来往	lái wǎng	come and go	
来信	lái xìn	incoming letters	
来源	lái yuán	source; origin	
来自	lái zi	come from	
来日方长	lái rì fāng cháng	there is ample time ahead	
出来	chū lái	come out	

Example:

这 些 水 果 是 来 自 澳 洲 的 。
Zhè xiē shuǐ guǒ shì lái zi Ào Zhōu de.

It means, "These fruits are from Australia."

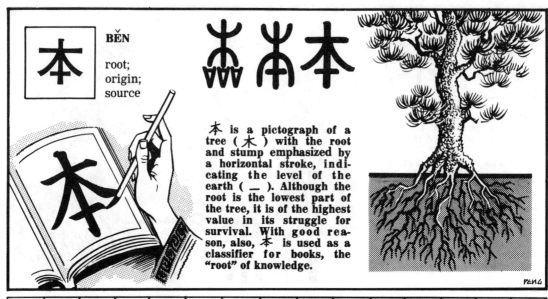

BĚN

root;
origin;
source

本 is a pictograph of a tree (木) with the root and stump emphasized by a horizontal stroke, indicating the level of the earth (⎯). Although the root is the lowest part of the tree, it is of the highest value in its struggle for survival. With good reason, also, 本 is used as a classifier for books, the "root" of knowledge.

一 十 才 木 本

本地	běn dì	this locality
本分	běn fèn	one's duty
本国	běn quó	one's own country
本行	běn háng	one's own profession
本来; 原本	běn lái; yuán běn	originally
本领	běn lǐng	skill; ability
本能	běn néng	instinct

本人	běn rén	I (me; myself)
本身	běn shēn	itself; in itself
本文	běn wén	this text
本性	běn xìng	natural instincts
本意	běn yì	original intention
本义	běn yì	original meaning
本质	běn zhì	innate character
本子	běn zi	book; notebook

Example:

这 件 事 情 根 本 和 我 无 关 。

Zhè jiàn shì qíng gēn běn hé wǒ wú guān.

It means, "This matter has nothing to do with me at all."

体 (體) ^{TǏ} the body

THE regular form: 體 combines 骨 (bone) with 豐 (plenty). The radical: 骨 itself is made up of skeleton (冎) and flesh (月). The other component: 豐 is a precious vessel symbolizing plenty. Hence: 體, meaning "body" from skeleton, flesh and plenty. The simplified form gets to the root (本) of man (亻), reducing him to a skeleton character: 体.

ノ 亻 亻 什 休 休 体

体裁	tǐ cái	types or forms of literature
体操	tǐ cāo	gymnastics
体罚	tǐ fá	physical punishment
体格	tǐ gé	physique; body
体会	tǐ huì	realise
体力	tǐ lì	physical (bodily) strength
体面	tǐ miàn	dignity; face
体贴	tǐ tiē	show consideration for
体统	tǐ tǒng	propriety; decency
体温	tǐ wēn	body temperature
体系	tǐ xì	system; set-up
体形	tǐ xíng	bodily form; build
体验	tǐ yàn	learn through practice
体育	tǐ yù	physical training
体重	tǐ zhòng	body weight

Example:

他 体 重 六 十 公 斤 。
Tā tǐ zhòng liù shí gōng jīn.
It means, "He weighs sixty kilograms."

果

GUǑ

fruit

THE earliest form was a stylised tree sporting a showy display of fruit: ✿. As it grew mighty, it boasted of more fruit: 櫐 but these are not easily discernible in the modern form: 果. The proverb provides a clue to the missing fruit: "Though a tree grows to a thousand feet, its fruits will fall to earth again."

丶 冂 冃 日 旦 甲 東 果

果断	guǒ duàn	resolute; decisive
果敢	guǒ gǎn	resolute and daring
果酱	guǒ jiàng	jam
果皮	guǒ pí	skin of fruit
果品	guǒ pǐn	fruit
果然	guǒ rán	as expected; sure enough

果肉	guǒ ròu	flesh of fruit
果实	guǒ shí	fruit; gain
果树	guǒ shù	fruit tree
果园	guǒ yuán	orchard
果汁	guǒ zhī	fruit juice
果子	guǒ zī	fruit

Example:

这 果 汁 太 甜 了 !

Zhè guǒ zhī tài tián le !

It means, "This fruit juice is too sweet!"

课（課）

KÈ lesson

課, meaning "lesson", is based on words (言) and fruit (果). A lesson (課) involves the use of words of instruction (言) to produce results, i.e., bear fruit (果). But, for words to be fruitful, take a lesson from the proverb: "Bitter words are medicine; sweet words bring illness."

丶 讠 讠 讠 讠 讠 讠 课 课 课

课本	kè běn	textbook
课程	kè chéng	course; curriculum
课堂; 课室	kè táng; kè shì	classroom
课外	kè wài	outside class
课文	kè wén	text
课余	kè yú	after school

课外活动	kè wài huó dòng	extra-curricular activities
功课	gōng kè	homework
上课	shàng kè	attend class
下课	xià kè	finish class
功课表	gōng kè biǎo	time-table

Example:

上 课 时 要 注 意 听 讲 。
Shàng kè shí yào zhù yì tīng jiǎng.
It means, "Please pay attention in class."

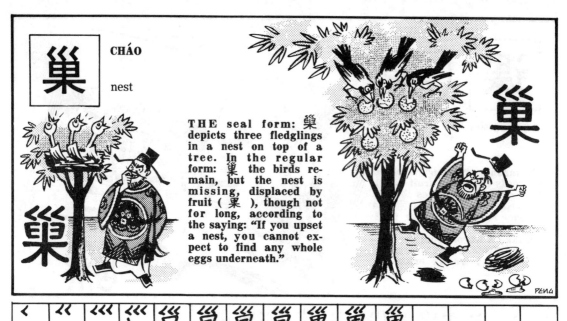

CHÁO

nest

THE seal form: 巢 depicts three fledglings in a nest on top of a tree. In the regular form: 巢 the birds remain, but the nest is missing, displaced by fruit (果), though not for long, according to the saying: "If you upset a nest, you cannot expect to find any whole eggs underneath."

〈　〈〈　〈〈〈　巛　씨　쎄　쎄　쎄　單　單　巢

巢穴	cháo xué	den; lair
匪巢	feǐ cháo	bandits' lair
鸟巢	niǎo cháo	bird's nest

Example:

树 上 有 一 个 鸟 巢 。
Shù shàng yǒu yí gè niǎo cháo .
It means, "There is a bird's nest on the tree."

166

MÒ

tip; end

JUST as the root (本) of a tree (木) is emphasized by a horizontal stroke (一) at its base, so the top of the tree (木) is indicated by a long horizontal line (一) at the top: 末, suggesting the tip or end - its limit. In growing upright like the tree, man also has his limit for, as the proverb puts it, "There are more trees upright than upright men."

| 一 | 二 | 才 | 才 | 末 | | | | | | | |

末代	mò dài	last reign of a dynasty
末后	mò hòu	finally
末了	mò liǎo	last; finally
末路	mò lù	dead end
末期	mò qī	last stage; final phase

末日	mò rì	end; doomsday
周末	zhōu mò	weekend
末流	mò liú	the later and decadent stage of a school of thoughts, etc.

Example:

他 喜 欢 在 周 末 带 孩 子 去 玩 。

Tā xǐ huān zài zhōu mò dài hái zi qù wán .

It means, "He likes to bring his children out during weekends."

未 WÈI

not; not yet

THIS character is to be distinguished from 末 (limit) in that the horizontal stroke across the top is much shorter: 未. In 末 the top line is emphasized; in 未 it is subdued, not fully grown. Hence 未 : not yet. Those who have "not yet" attained their end should exercise patience and take heart from the proverb: "A giant tree grows from a tiny bud."

一 二 十 才 未

未必	wèi bì	not necessarily; may not
未曾	wèi céng	have not; never
未定	wèi dìng	uncertain; undecided
未婚	wèi hūn	unmarried

未来	wèi lái	future
未完	wèi wán	unfinished
未详	wèi xiáng	unknown
未知数	wèi zhī shù	unknown number
未雨绸缪	wèi yǔ chóu móu	take precautions

Example:

他 对 未 来 感 到 茫 然 。

Tā duì wèi lái gǎn dào máng rán.

It means, "He is at a loss over his future."

168

妹

MÈI

younger sister

未, the phonetic, is a tree in full leaf and branch, but not fully mature and means: "not". With the addition of the radical for girl (女), the character for "younger sister" is formed. Hence 妹: a girl (女) who has not yet (未) reached maturity.

く 女 女 女⁻ 女= 女† 妹 妹

| 妹夫 | mèi fū | younger sister's husband |
| 妹妹 | mèi mei | younger sister |

| 表妹 | biǎo mèi | younger female cousin |

Example:

我 的 表 妹 长 得 很 漂 亮 。

Wǒ de biǎo mèi zhǎng de hěn piào liàng.

It means, "My cousin is very pretty."

姐 JIĚ

elder sister

女 is the radical for girl or woman. 且, the phonetic, is a picture of a stool (冂) with two rungs (=), standing on the ground (一), now borrowed for the conjunction: 且 "moreover". In our picture, the stool is not the only thing that distinguishes older sister from younger sister.

| 姐夫 | jiě fū | elder sister's husband | 姐妹 | jiě mèi | sisters |
| 姐姐 | jiě jie | elder sister | 表姐 | biǎo jiě | elder female cousin |

Example:

我 的 姐 姐 喜 欢 吃 榴 梿 。
Wǒ de jiě jie xǐ huān chī liú lián.
It means, "My elder sister likes durians."

爱 (愛) ÀI
love; affection

THE regular form: 愛 is made up of 旡 (breathe into), 心 (heart) and 夂 (gracious motion), implying that what gives breath to the heart and inspires gracious motion is love — an idealistic love. The simplifed form: 爱 highlights the role of friendship: 友 (hand 𠂇 in hand 又 co-operation) — a more realistic love. But whatever form love may take, none can excel the selfless and unselfish love based on the principle extolled in the proverb: "Those who love others will themselves be loved."

ノ ⺈ ⺈ ⺈ ⺈ ⺈ 旡 旡 爱 爱 爱

爱国	ài guó	patriotic
爱好	ài hào	interest; hobby
爱护	ài hù	cherish; take good care of
爱怜	ài lián	show tender affection for
爱恋	ài liàn	be in love with
爱慕	ài mù	adore; admire

爱情	ài qíng	love (between man and woman)
爱人	ài rén	sweetheart
爱惜	ài xī	treasure; cherish
爱憎	ài zēng	love and hate
爱尔兰	Ài'Ěr Lán	Ireland
爱不释手	ài bù shì shǒu	fondle admiringly

Example:

小 梅 喜 欢 看 爱 情 小 说 。

Xiǎo Méi xǐ huān kàn ài qíng xiǎo shuō.

It means, "Xiao Mei likes to read romances."

171

想

XIĂNG

think; hope

THIS character is composed of 相 (inspect) and 心 (heart). The phonetic: 相 represents an eye (目) behind a tree (木) on the lookout for possible danger, and signifies to examine or inspect. Combination with the radical: 心 (heart, mind) produces 想, meaning to examine or inspect in the heart or mind, i.e., to think, ponder or hope.

| 一 | 十 | 才 | 木 | 利 | 机 | 相 | 相 | 相 | 相 | 想 | 想 | 想 | |

想到	xiǎng dào	think of; call to mind	想起	xiǎng qǐ	recall	
想法	xiǎng fǎ	think of a way; what one has in mind	想象	xiǎng xiàng	imagine; fancy	
			想不到	xiǎng bu dào	unexpected	
			想不开	xiǎng bu kāi	take things too hard; take a matter to heart	
想来	xiǎng lái	it may be assumed that				
			想当然	xiǎng dāng rán	take for granted	
想念	xiǎng niàn	remember with longing; miss	想得开	xiǎng de kāi	not take to heart	
			想入非非	xiǎng rù fēi fēi	indulge in fantasy	

Example:

我 想 我 该 走 了 。

Wǒ xiǎng wǒ gāi zǒu le.

It means, "I'm afraid I must be going now."

172

忆 (憶)

YÌ   recall; remember; reflect

THE phonetic: 意 denotes sound (音) in the heart or mind (心), i.e., intention or thought. The addition of another heart (the radical 忄) to thought (意) suggests to think again — to reflect or remember: 憶. As a mnemonic aid, the simplified form combines heart (忄) with second (乙) producing 忆.

丶	忄	忄	忆								

回忆	huí yì	recollect	
记忆	jì yì	remember	
记忆力	jì yì lì	memory	

记忆犹新	jì yì yóu xīn	remain fresh in one's memory

Example:

我 的 记 忆 力 很 差 。
Wǒ de jì yì lì hěn chà.
It means, "My memory is very poor."

WÀNG

忘

forget

THE old form of the phonetic: 亡 represents someone entering (入) a place of concealment (ㄴ), and means to disappear or perish: (亡). The addition of the heart radical: 心 enforces the idea of "lost mind" or a mind that ceases to act; hence, to forget: 忘. Minds should not be lost when it comes to the memorable proverb: "Forget favours given: remember favours received."

丶 亠 亡 亡 忘 忘 忘

忘本	wàng běn	forget one's origin	
忘掉	wàng diào	forget	
忘怀	wàng huái	forget	
忘记	wàng jì	forget	
忘情	wàng qíng	be unmoved	
忘我	wàng wǒ	selfless	

忘形	wàng xíng	be beside oneself
忘年交	wàng nián jiāo	friendship between generations
忘恩负义	wàng'ēn fù yì	ungrateful
健忘	jiàn wàng	forgetful

Example:

别 忘 记 替 我 买 水 果 。

Bié wàng jì tì wǒ mǎi shuǐ guǒ.

It means, "Don't forget to buy fruits for me."

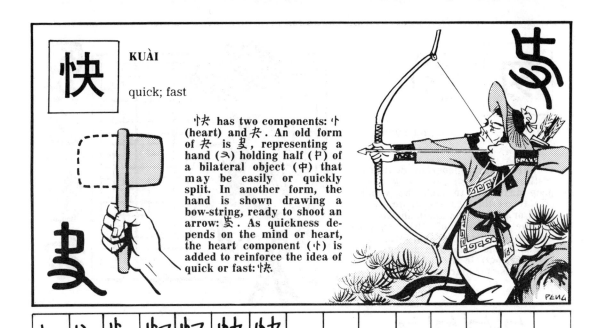

快 KUÀI

quick; fast

快 has two components: 忄 (heart) and 夬. An old form of 夬 is 叏, representing a hand (彐) holding half (卩) of a bilateral object (中) that may be easily or quickly split. In another form, the hand is shown drawing a bow-string, ready to shoot an arrow: 叏. As quickness depends on the mind or heart, the heart component (忄) is added to reinforce the idea of quick or fast: 快.

丶	八	忄	忄ㄱ	忄乛	忄夬	快					

快步	kuài bù	trot	快乐	kuài lè	happy
快餐	kuài cān	quick meal; snack	快慢	kuài màn	speed
快车	kuài chē	express train or bus	快速	kuài sù	fast
快感	kuài gǎn	pleasant sensation	快艇	kuài tǐng	speedboat
快活	kuài huó	merry	快马加鞭	kuài mǎ jiā biān	at high speed

Example:

我 有 一 个 快 乐 的 家 庭 。
Wǒ yǒu yí gè kuài lè de jiā tíng.
It means, "I have a happy family."

175

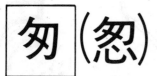

CŌNG   haste; hurry; alarm

THE original ideograph depicted a restless heart (心) prompting one to peep anxiously through the window (囪). Hence the meaning: haste, excitement or alarm. The haste shown even in the evolution of this exciting character — from the seal form: 悤 to 悤 and 忩 and, with utter disregard for the heart (心), in the final form: 匆 — gives cause for alarm.

匆匆	cōng cōng	hurriedly
匆促	cōng cù	hastily
匆忙	cōng máng	hastily; hurriedly

Example:

他 匆 匆 吃 了 早 餐 便 上 学 。

Tā cōng cōng chī le zǎo cān biàn shàng xué.

It means, "After hurrying through his breakfast, he went to school."